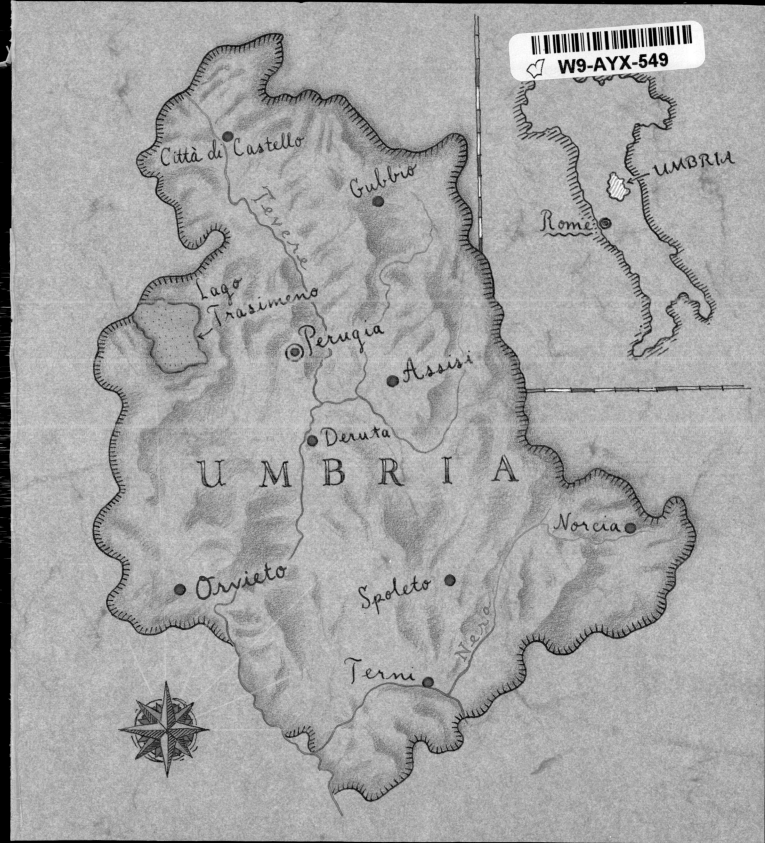

Città di Castello

Gubbio

Tevere

Lago
Trasimeno

Perugia

Assisi

Deruta

U M B R I A

Orvieto

Spoleto

Norcia

Nera

Terni

Roma

UMBRIA

Julia della Croce's

UMBRIA

Regional Recipes from the Heartland of Italy

PHOTOGRAPHS BY JOHN RIZZO

CHRONICLE BOOKS

SAN FRANCISCO

Dedicated to my father,
GIOVANNI DELLA CROCE,
from whence comes the wanderlust.

Text copyright © 2002 by Julia della Croce.
Photographs copyright © 2002 by John A. Rizzo.

Library of Congress Cataloging-in-Publication Data:

Della Croce, Julia.
    Julia della Croce's Umbria / by Julia della Croce; photo-
        graphs by John A. Rizzo.
        p. cm.
    Includes index.
    ISBN 0-8118-2351-2 (pbk.)
    1. Cookery, Italian. 2. Cookery—Italy—Umbria. 3. Umbria
        (Italy)—History. I. Title.

TX723.D3973 2002
641.5945'65—dc21

Manufactured in Singapore.

Designed by Stuart McKee Design, San Francisco
Typeset in Filosofia and Trade Gothic

Distributed in Canada by Raincoast Books
9050 Shaughnessy Street
Vancouver, BC V6P 6E5

10 9 8 7 6 5 4 3 2 1

Chronicle Books LLC
85 Second Street
San Francisco, California 94105

www.chroniclebooks.com

In Memoriam
In memoriam to Thomas Briccetti, conductor, composer, *buon gustaio*, friend. Born 1932, New York. Died 1999, Perugia. How will you live in all eternity without *spaghetti alla norcina?* Who can think of drinking the beautiful wines you left in your cellar without you? If we opened them, would we hear a scented song? If we drank them, would we be flush with your laughter? Perhaps the Mysterious One has concocted a special dew for you. Here's to you. May you infect the next world, too, with your joie de vivre, and play it on the stage of all eternity.

Photographer's Acknowledgments
The photographer wishes to thank Cathy Whimms, chef/owner of Genoa Restaurant in Portland, Oregon, for her dedication to the recipes while preparing the wonderful food photographed for this book. Cathy is not a food stylist, but an extraordinarily talented, nationally recognized chef who is passionate about Italian food. She prepared the food in this book as if it were to be served to the guests at Genoa Restaurant.

    Also, a special thank you to Donna Macdonald and David West for their many trips to the markets in and around Perugia and their tireless efforts in collecting the pottery and props for the photographs.

    Thank yous must be given to Martha Boyden and her beautiful villa Colle San Giorgio, a restored farmhouse located in the hills outside of Perugia. The food was photographed in and around the villa. Colle San Giorgio is available for rentals by contacting marthaboyden@mclink.it or Italia Reservations.

Table of Contents

Introduction

Dubbed "the green and sacred land" after Saint Francis, Saint Rita, and other celebrated Umbrian holy figures, Umbria is steeped in mysticism and tradition. This lush and hilly region, Italy's geographical heart, is distinguished by the shadows of its dark forests and the rugged mountains that cover over half of its land area. On Umbria's southern borders rise the Sibilline Mountains, while to the east lies the stark spine of the Apennines. Journalist Waverley Root called Umbria "a land of swiftly rising heights and deep valleys, with landscapes alternately smiling and savage." The thousand valleys are specked with castles and villas. The walled medieval cities immortalized by Giotto, Lorenzetti, Perugino, and Pinturicchio jut out of tufa rock into the dreamy skyline.

FACING PAGE:
Casteluccio fields

Rivers, lakes, and streams glitter everywhere and connect the ups and downs. The green, fertile valleys of the Tiber and the Nera encourage cattle and pig farming, grain and vegetable crops, and olive groves. Trasimeno, Bolsena, and smaller lakes provide fishing. The mountains' shadows protect the land from parching in the hot months, making it green in deep summer, not brown the way it is in Tuscany to the west and in Lazio to the south, while the forests on the hilly slopes bear wild mushrooms, asparagus, and herbs in profusion. Umbria is more rugged than Tuscany, more forested, less cultivated, and more wild, but in every way as spectacular. If it has been in Tuscany's shadow, it has been so only because of a certain resistance to outsiders, a certain contemplativeness.

ETRURIA AT TABLE

Umbrian culture and cuisine reflect the historical and geographical isolation of the region's past and present. The Etruscans, who called their country Etruria, flourished throughout central Italy, with their civilization reaching its apex of wealth and power in the sixth century B.C. Valleys were planted with the same mother crops grown in Umbria today, particularly olives, grapes, and *farro*, an ancient grain that predates common wheat and now is making a comeback. In 295 B.C., when the Romans penetrated, Etruscan culture was already highly developed. It was easy for the invaders to conquer Etruria, because its centers were widely scattered, but the ancients' zest for life and the refinement and naturalness of their culture survived the Roman conquest, the barbarian hordes, and the Dark Ages. Umbria's spiritual life, language, and cuisine are still Etruscan at heart.

Many writers and philosophers, from ancient times to the present, have been taken with what the contemporary Italian scholar, Massimo Pallottino, calls "Etruscomania." From Virgil, Pliny, and Horace to D. H. Lawrence and Aldous Huxley, all who have rested an elbow on the philosopher's stone have given the mysterious Etruscans a mythical status.

What is it about these people that has made them the stuff of legend? A view of their world can be seen from the lively carvings on their death vaults. Theirs was a peaceful and sensuous culture that held that human pleasures were symbolic gestures linking the life of the flesh with the life of the spirit. No civilization could fit more perfectly a romantic's view of an ideal society: one unfettered by customs and laws; that elevated rather than repressed elemental human desires, and permitted—even glorified—their open expression.

[In Umbria] one believes he is dreaming or finding himself in front of theatrical scenery and needs to persuade himself continually that instead, everything is there, firm and fixed in the stone.

—MARIA LAURA DELLA CROCE,
Umbria: lungo i sentieri dell'arte e dello spirito

In this profoundly spiritual life, natural objects held symbolic meaning, joining the seen with the unseen. Food and wine were sacred vehicles that transmuted the soul from the material life into the eternal, providing pleasure during the journey. Sumptuous banquets were held twice a day in those households that could afford it. Every meal began with a salutation and a toast to Phuphluns, the Etruscan deity. While the meal was eaten in a reclining position, someone always arose during the feasting to recount the origins of life and to carry on conversations with the Eternal. It was customary to eat not one course, but many, one after another, in order to extend the pleasures of the table. Food was consumed in the company of loved ones and friends, in an atmosphere of music and dance and lively conversation.

The Etruscan kitchen used a combination of ingredients to create a harmony of flavors, paralleling the formula necessary for community well-being. Even the most intensely flavored aromatics, such as mint, rue, pepper, and mustard, were united skillfully to deliver a gentle effect. Wine accompanied everything and flowed abundantly.

While the Romans prized the martial arts, the Etruscans valued pleasure. It was natural for male servants to be naked while on duty in the banquet hall, a practice that diners believed created a heightened sense of physical enjoyment, aesthetic pleasure, and conviviality. The uninhibited celebration of emotions and natural human functions baffled all but the poets among the Romans. Some Romans considered the Etruscans depraved.

Certain Etruscan culinary traditions continue to this day in Umbria. The most important of these is the natural, simple approach to cooking that is handed down from mother to daughter, rather than through great cooking schools or famous chefs. Then, as now, the kitchen was based on olive oil, both for cooking and for anointing and flavoring food after cooking, and roasting and grilling were the preferred methods of preparing meat and fish. Variety meats, such as liver, lung, heart, and kidney, were chopped and made into a sausage called *budellina*, and eggs, a symbol of life, had an elevated status on the table, appearing before the

serving of the first and second courses. The daily diet of the relatively affluent consisted of domesticated meats and wild game, including *porchetta* (roasted suckling pig), chicken, goose, duck, pheasant, boar, venison, many small game birds, grains, chestnuts and other nuts, honey, cheeses, fruits, and vegetables. Etruscans were great saltwater fishermen (Etruria was a powerful force in maritime trade), but they also prized the freshwater fish of their lakes and streams, just as Umbrians do today. Wild herbs, garlic, and onions, which flourished on the land-scape, were important both for flavoring and for health.

CONTEMPORARY UMBRIAN COOKING

Anyone who has read the history of Roman cookery knows that *garum* was a fermented fish sauce that cooks used indiscriminately. The Etruscans used it, too, as a piquant flavoring for meat dishes, particularly game. The penchant for the gastronomical sting that began with *garum* has evolved into the use of vinegar, both in cooking or as a condiment, in counterpoint to fruity olive oil. The bite of vinegar, or the cleansing of the palate with wine, refreshes and prolongs the desire for unctuous taste sensations course after course. At a lecture in Trevi, where he teaches, legendary Umbrian-born chef Angelo Paracucchi explained that the foundation of genuine Italian cooking is built on three ingredients: olive oil, wine, and vinegar. Perhaps nothing better describes the essence of contemporary Umbrian taste.

Umbrian cooking is exquisitely simple. For that very reason, its ingredients must be excellent, as they often stand alone. The maxim is obvious for a region that has relied on the products from the fields and forests of which it is primarily comprised.

What else distinguishes Umbrian cooking? Its flavors are akin to winter colors: pure, assertive, direct, clear as glass. The food is honest, although scented with local herbs and aromatics. These are used lavishly, even extravagantly, but always to complement other ingredients. The unpretentious marriage of the heady earth flavors of black truffles and wild mushrooms to meat and game is made in the same simple spirit.

FACING PAGE:
A typical Umbrian *trattoria*

Then there is the grassroots revival of once-forgotten legumes and grains such as native lentils and *farro*, which are being used in new and imaginative ways. The recurring elements are the delicious olive oil; the perfumes of wild fennel, rosemary, sage, and juniper; the bite of garlic and zesty local capers; green and black olives; sweet and bitter almonds and pine nuts; the splendid hams, salamis, sausages, and artfully cured pork cuts of the famous butchers of Norcia; the *battuto* (the vegetable-and-herb flavor base of many dishes) of pork fat, marjoram, and garlic that initiates soups, sauces, and stuffings; pungent fresh sheep's milk cheeses; and the rich, smoky flavors of goose, game birds, boar, and venison. All play a role in the diet. So, too, does the delicate, sweet flesh of lakefish contrasted with the savory stuffings of herbs, onion, and bacon; earthy, dense black truffles; creamy-fleshed local potatoes; thick heads of deep emerald native celery; fat bulbs of sweet fennel; and toothsome pastas of *farro* and wheat flour. Good local red and white wines are always in the pantry and on the table.

Umbria is atypical of other central and southern Italian regions in that its cuisine is meat oriented. Also atypical is its propensity for cooking as much as possible over a fire, on a grill, or in an oven, rather than stove-top cooking, which predominates in other parts of the country. In past times, the Umbrian oven was first fired up for baking bread, then, in order to make use of the heat, it was used for roasting meats. When the oven cooled, it was employed for drying fruits. Pasta is not held in the esteem here that it is in the south, nor is rice or polenta, both obsessions in the northern regions. Still, all three appear as first-course foods on the Umbrian table, and so do soups, which are often more substantial than in other regions. In Umbria, soups are often thickened with *farro*, chickling peas, chickpeas, or lentils, their use no doubt an influence of the region's traditional hearty mountain cooking.

Provincial culinary variations abound. The Perugian journalist L. Chiari Guardabassi describes them as *"al di là del lago"* (beyond the lake [Trasimeno]) and *"al di là dei monti Martani"* (beyond the Martani Mountains). The Trasimeno kitchen takes fish seriously, pairing them

The Amazon forest is the world's oxygen reservoir. Umbria performs the same function for Italy.

—L'Etichetta, March 1993

with the limpid oils that are pressed from the olive harvests within the lake's gentle microclimate. The cities and towns in the lake district, Passignano sul Trasimeno and Castiglione del Lago, for instance, have grown around the local fishing cultures.

To the east are the provinces that lie within the Nera Valley and the Sibilline Mountains. Here, under the Spoleto and Norcia soil, are found the tastiest black truffles in the world. The food is mountain food: stick-to-the-ribs lentil dishes, sheep's milk cheese, lamb roasted with mountain herbs, stewed game of many varieties.

The countryside to the north and west shares a border with Tuscany, and the cooking shows it. This is the only part of Umbria where one finds beef, for which, of course, neighboring Tuscany is famous. Some of the border areas even cook with Tuscan olive oil, which is more "peppery" than the mellow Umbrian oils. As in the rest of Italy, the olive oil has its own distinctions, resulting from local subtleties of climate and landscape, whose nuances are discernible to the natives.

Perugia's fiercely independent past and the international influences of its present make its cooking somewhat eclectic. It has its own specialties nevertheless. The city lives in two psychological worlds: one is global in outlook, and the other, formed by its proud and defiant history, is inward-looking and rich in tradition.

To the south, in the lower Tiber Valley, the temperate days and the cool, breezy nights that discourage the dreaded olive fly provide an ideal climate for making the area's legendary oil and superb wine.

Further distinctions exist, typically small details, such as one part of a province sautés sausages with white grapes while the other side sautés them with black grapes, or that Todi makes their anise biscotti with white flour, while Perugia blends in buckwheat. Orvieto, a jewel on the crown of Terni, has been famous since antiquity for its white wine, and the province has its own cooking style. The local kitchen is known for its *insaccati*, meat "puddings," and its game fowl baked into yeast pies. Because Terni borders Lazio to the south, it shares some of that region's predilection for fiery food, although the farther north into the province one travels, the less pepper one finds. Bevagna, in the province of Perugia and comparatively far from the border of Lazio, nevertheless cooks in the Roman style because it was once an important strategic Roman encampment.

Modern Umbrian food is based on an ancient culture of refined simplicity, and a timeless quality persists in Umbrian cooking even today. Take for example the instructions for cooking pizza in La signora Guglielma Corsi's classic postwar cookbook, *Un secolo di cucina umbra*, still the Umbrian housewife's cooking bible. She tells us, if we can, to bring the flat bread to a fireplace and to slide it onto an iron tripod, a method that conjures medieval and Renaissance woodcuts of cooks baking loaves in an open hearth over a slab of stone. Why continue these traditions that mean nothing to so many modern people? Because, Corsi writes, "My mind returns gratefully to remembering those who came before us, deprived of all kinds of conveniences, who handed down in an original manner what was authentic and really special."

Thus, the past must be understood in order to understand the present and its culinary corollary: Umbrian food is best appreciated when eaten at a rustic table in a room warmed by a fire and facing a distant view.

Come to marvel at it, all of you.

—Ruggero Grieco, Umbria

FACING PAGE:
La signora Guglielma Corsi, legendary Umbrian cook and author of *La cucina umbra*

Umbrian Wines

vini umbri

Until thirty years ago, it was customary among farmers and country people to offer guests and travelers a glass of wine to drink with the proviso that the last few drops be spilled on the floor as a benediction.

—Rita Boini, Umbrian culinary writer

There is no question that viticulture in Umbria has its roots in Etruria. Workers tilling the soil in Torgiano today to prepare it for new grape cuttings are still unearthing the remains of Etruscan wine amphorae. A respect for this rich past continues to prevail in contemporary wine making.

My friend Bill Marsano, an award-winning wine writer, has noted that "If Umbria has lagged behind, has not become a 'technologically advanced wine-making center,' neither has she become a wine culture of suits and BMWs, gas chromatographs, and stainless-steel tank farms that look like oil refineries. Umbrians have not rushed headlong to uproot vast tracts of traditional vines and replace them wholesale with Cabernet, Chardonnay, and other dreaded international varieties," he says. "Wine here—a staple, not a fetish—remains close to its roots in peasant agriculture."

Wine is a profound part of the fabric of daily life and a vital part of every meal, whether for the peasant, who makes his own for his family's consumption, or the city dweller, who drives out to the countryside to buy it *vendita diretta*, "direct from the home cellar." Wine is, in fact, nothing short of a sacred drink.

Orvieto has been famous for its white wine since Etruscan and Roman times, when its wines were transported as far north as Gaul and the Nordic countries. In modern times, the Lungarotti and Antinori cellars have become almost household words to even the uninitiated wine drinker. That other Umbrian wines have not been heard of outside the borders of Italy—or of Umbria, for that matter—doesn't mean that the region has not produced wines of distinction. The Sagrantino of Montefalco, for example, both *secco* (dry) and *passito* (red wine made from partially dried, thus sweeter grapes), was an exclusive wine drunk only by the noble families of Montefalco until the 1940s. According to Umbrian culinary writer Rita Boini, the making of Sagrantino *passito* was a rite that every important family of Montefalco knew and followed but kept secret, partly due to local mandate and partly due to tradition.

Only in recent years have more of Umbria's exceptional wines become known outside the region. Arnaldo Caprai is an Umbrian vintner whose wines have starred in Italian competitions and more than held their own next to the better-known Umbrian labels. Còlpetrone, Adanti, Antano, Antonelli, and Bea are not far behind. These wines are exported to America.

Wines of quality are produced throughout Umbria, but there are nine restricted DOC (Denominazione di Origine Controllata) zones. They are Assisi, Colli Altotiberini, Colli Amerini, Colli del Trasimeno, the zone of Torgiano, Colli Perugini, the zone of Montefalco, Colli Martani, and the zone of Orvieto.

Labels indicating these DOC zones are worth seeking out, for when eating Umbrian dishes, one should bring the earth, sun, and anima— the "soul"—that is captured in its wines to the table, too.

The Umbrian Pantry

la dispensa umbra

While some of the ingredients listed here are found in other regions, Umbria has its own variations based on local tradition. Even cheeses and *salumi* with the same names elsewhere are produced according to Umbrian tastes. Of course, not all of these ingredients are available outside of the region. But anyone who is seriously interested in reproducing authentic Umbrian flavors should at least have a textbook understanding of the palette of colors—that is, the genuine products.

Cheeses The Castelluccio plain in the Norcia basin, grazing land for cattle and sheep, is the source of milk for Umbrian cheeses, both fresh and aged, and other dairy products. Aged pecorino (*pecora* means sheep), which is used outside of Italy as a grating cheese, is well-known in America. Far less familiar is fresh sheep's cheese (*caciotta*), a simple but delicious eating cheese. Although sophisticated modern cheese-making methods have replaced many traditional, labor-intensive artisanal practices as a means of meeting government standards for hygiene, Umbrian cheese makers continue to produce the same traditional *formaggi*.

FACING PAGE:
Norcineria Muscattelli— store worker

Fresh cheeses must be eaten within a day or so of being made. Although not as perishable, aged Umbrian cheeses reach American tables in only the smallest numbers, so travelers should seek out cheese shops and restaurants in Umbria for an authentic taste of the region. Very soft fresh cheeses such as ricotta and mascarpone are used in pasta sauces and desserts, just as they are in other parts of Italy. Solidified soft cheeses are table cheeses, but in Umbria they are also grilled or baked. Grilled or baked cheeses are more prevalent in summer, when sweet tomatoes or fresh greens are at hand to serve alongside them, and then they are offered as antipasti or as a single course for a meatless or light meal.

Caciotta: Produced on farms in the Apennines, *caciotta* is made from a combination of cow's and sheep's milk. The rind is thin, smooth, and cream colored, while the cheese itself is ivory colored and firm but semisoft. The sheep's milk makes it tangy, but it retains a pleasantly clear, buttery flavor from the cow's milk, as long as the cheese is not aged too long. Longer-aged *caciotta* is stronger in flavor.

Cheese with black truffle: Also produced in the Umbrian Apennines, this distinctive fresh cheese is a combination of cow's and sheep's milk into which small pieces of crushed truffle are mixed.

Mascarpone: This sweet, soft, creamy fresh cheese is particularly pleasant because of the wholesomeness of the region's cow's milk.

Mozzarella: In Umbria, mozzarella is produced from cow's milk. It is a fresh cheese, meant to be eaten on the same day it is made. It is soft, round or oval, and with a thin, glassy skin that is formed in layers. Unlike the fresh cow's milk version made in America, the flavor is mildly and pleasantly acidic due to the natural lactic fermenting agents that are added to the milk to enrich it.

Pecorino: Sheep's milk cheeses are produced in the hills of Norcia, Cascia, Preci, Spoleto, Gualdo Todino, Fossato di Vico, and Gubbio. The sharp, tangy flavor of typical sheep's milk cheese is tempered in Umbrian pecorino by the mountain pastures filled with aquatic cresses, wild celery, and other vegetation on which the animals graze. Umbrian pecorino is safe from the torrid heat and parched vegetation that is typical of Sardinia and Lazio, Italy's largest producers of pecorino. The cheese has a thin, smooth, orange rind, is creamy white and faintly riddled with holes, and has a pleasant and mild flavor. It is made in one of two ways, depending on whether the outcome is to be a fresh cheese or an aged one. For fresh pecorino, which is eaten after thirty days of maturing and is soft, the temperature of the milk is kept low and the curds are broken down roughly. Pecorino that is marked for aging is made from milk heated to a higher temperature and the curds are broken into a finer texture. One of the best ways to serve the aged type is to slice it, top the slices with some black truffle, and warm the cheese in a very hot oven for 2 minutes until melted, then top with more truffle.

Ravigiolo: A fresh, soft, crumbly cow's milk cheese, *ravigiolo* is flat and cylindrical. As it is not aged, it has a fresh flavor and no rind.

Ricotta: Made from cow's milk, sheep's milk, or a mixture, ricotta is made in rush baskets. It is used in baking, or it is eaten fresh, sometimes sprinkled with sugar and cinnamon for breakfast, or eaten by children as a snack.

Smoked scamorza and provola: These ripened cow's milk cheeses have thin, smooth, cream-colored rinds. They are used in cooking or eaten as table cheese.

Chickling Peas

Chickling peas, or *cicèrchie*, are a type of grass pea. They are different from chickpeas, being smaller, squatter, and somewhat square in comparison, and their flavor can be described as a cross between chickpeas and fava beans. Like many legumes and grains used in Umbria today, *cicèrchie* vanished during the postwar shift toward modernization, when many traditional foods fell out of use. They have been rediscovered and developed for modern production, farmed mainly in the Colfiorito area.

In cooking, *cicèrchie* are used much the way chickpeas and fava beans are, in soups or boiled and dressed with rich local olive oil (see Etruscan Soup, page 72). The flour of the chickling pea is the basis for *cicerchiata*, a fried carnival sweet coated with honey and candy sprinkles or sliced almonds, variations of which can be found from Umbria all the way south to Abruzzo.

Farro

Chewing farro *is more work than chewing a hamburger, so it is good for our digestive system. . . .The grains cook quickly, too, which makes them especially good for men, because they always want to do things in a hurry.*

—Clarisse Schiller,
Campello sul Clitunno

Farro is emmer wheat in English, although it is often mistakenly called spelt. This mountain grain is another food that became nearly extinct after World War II. It is a familiar staple in Umbria today, cultivated in the Colfiorito area along with chickling peas and lentils. Farro is sold in its whole berry form; milled into flour for *umbricelli*, the handmade pasta specialty; or milled into medium and coarse grinds for soups and other dishes. It can be hard to find in food markets, but Italian food-specialty shops and well-stocked health-food stores have always carried it for its high fiber and considerable nutritional value.

Lentils

The Sibilline Mountains are a theatrical backdrop to the Castelluccio plain, which rises four thousand feet above sea level about halfway up the Apennines. In the fertile plain, which is said to resemble the Tibetan landscape, grow the lentils of Castelluccio, legumes renowned for their tiny size and exceptional flavor. The lentils have always been cultivated organically, not in response to modern sensibilities, but in keeping with age-old local traditions. The soil has a high clay content, which contributes to the rich, earthy flavor of the lentils. The success of the crops is ensured by local methods of crop rotation, in which the fields are planted with lentils one year, wheat the next, and the third year left fallow. This three-year planting cycle, which protects the fertility of the land, has been repeated for centuries. I have been pleasantly surprised to find these marvelous lentils in American food-specialty shops, but even supermarket-variety lentils will do nicely in Umbrian dishes if high-quality extra-virgin olive oil is used for cooking and flavoring.

Mushrooms

Among the species of wild mushrooms that grow in Umbria are the porcini, which begin to erupt from beneath the forest carpets during the first days of August. The mushroom season begins at the higher elevations first: The *russule*, porcini, and *prataioli* grow at about eighteen hundred feet.

Then follow the *ovoli* and the *gialli galletti* on the lower hills among the chestnut groves. By November, the *sanguinosi* (bloody ones) appear in the pine forests. Wild mushrooms begin to make their appearance in local markets and restaurants on the same day they are picked, when they are still juicy and quivering with the full range of their earthy flavor. The pungent wild mushrooms are important in the cooking of the region. Fortunately for us, harvesting and dehydrating porcini for later use and foreign export is as serious a business in Umbria as it is elsewhere in Italy.

MEAT SPECIALTIES *Cured Meats* The cured meats, or *salumi*, typical of Umbria are made primarily in the Norcia area and in the mountainous zones of the upper Tiber Valley as far north as Nocera Umbra and Gubbio.

Norcia *prosciutto crudo*—"raw" air-cured ham—is the pride of all Umbrian salumi. Like the region's bread and Umbrian food in general, it contains little salt. A long and tragic tale brought about this practice of undersalting. The Papacy controlled much of what went on in Perugia and its surroundings with little discord until 1305. In that year, in a minor dispute, Perugians opened fire on the Pope's army. That action—and the Pope's reaction—resulted in centuries of open rebellion by the Perugians against the Church. In 1538, the Church, in retaliation for the continuous hostility, levied a tax on salt, monopolized the salt beds, and forced all subjects to buy salt from pontifical stashes. The Perugians fought back but lost, and salt, which was essential for curing and preserving meat, especially prosciutto and other *salumi*, became nearly unattainable.

During the saltless years of battle and defeat, the famed pork butchers of Norcia developed a way to make prosciutto and other cured meats with as little salt as possible as a way to spite the Pope. The Umbrians contend that the secret was stolen by Parma, whose silky hams are the most celebrated in the world. Curing pork for *salumi* has become an art form in Norcia, so much so that the word *norcino* has come to mean "pork butcher" in Italian.

The high altitude and fresh mountain air of Norcia and the Valnerina are ideal conditions for curing prosciutto. Umbrian prosciutto is known as mountain ham precisely because it is cured at high altitudes in rooms well-ventilated by fresh mountain breezes. Unlike the famous prosciutti of Parma and San Daniele, the exposed surface of Umbrian hams is not covered with a thick protective rind, but instead treated to a generous dose of black pepper. The ham is hung and air-cured for one to two years. The one-year ham is called *prosciutto tipico di Norcia*, while the two-year ham, carefully made according to traditional artisanal methods, is a prized and precious product. A familiar saying of Norcia insists that "a good ham must go through at least one winter and one summer." This distinction is bestowed only upon the two-year ham. It can be distinguished from other prosciutti by a number of other characteristics as well, including its pearlike shape, which is arrived at by cutting the leg at right angles or, in other words, by making a U-shaped cut a palm's length away from the "knob" (thigh-bone joint), instead of the cut being made an inch or so away as is customary with other hams. The curing time is also longer and more complex than that of most hams.

The Norcia prosciutto never sees the blade of a meat slicer, but must be cut with a sharp knife by a skilled cutter. Eaten alone with bread, undisturbed by sweet intrusions of melon or figs and such, it is a revelation. Its uses in cooking are innumerable and unequaled as a flavor component to build a sauce, fortify a soup or risotto, or marry with other meats and vegetables.

In addition to prosciutto, Umbrians make the usual fresh and dried Italian sausages, *capocollo* (boned pork neck cured with salt, sugar, pepper, nutmeg or cloves, and white wine), *coppa* (a superb headcheese), and *lonza* (cured pork loin), but the region has its own cured pork specialties.

Budellacci di Norcia: Also called *noia* or *annoia*, meaning "boredom" or "boring," these sausages are made throughout Umbria, but they are a vestige of ancient Norcia custom and a specialty of that area. The entrails of specially reared pigs are meticulously washed with water and, usually, vinegar, wine, or lemon juice, and then seasoned with salt, pepper, and dill or aniseed. They are then hung to dry under a hot chimney for three to four days. *Budellacci* are grilled before they are eaten.

Corallina di Norcia: An Umbrian sausage so popular that it is even found elsewhere in Italy, *corallina* is a finely minced mixture of three-quarters top-quality pork and one-quarter pork fat, which gives the sausage its characteristic white dots when sliced. The seasoning consists of salt, peppercorns, and garlic marinated in wine. After it is stuffed into casings, the sausage is air-dried in a naturally well-ventilated room that is heated with a wood-burning stove stoked with hardwood and large quantities of juniper berries. After it is briefly smoked in this way, it is hung and aged in a cool, damp cellar for three to five months.

Mortadella: *Conoscitori* consider the mortadellas of Norcia, Cascia, and Preci to have no equal. They are made by blending finely ground top-quality pork meat from pigs that have been pampered and fed on horse chestnuts and acorns with salt, pepper, pistachios, and a secret spice formula. The huge sausage is then packed into a natural casing and a long strip of the tasty lard is inserted in the middle. Next it is pressed into a cylindrical shape, cooked, and hung for several days in a hot, airy room. After that, it is aged for five to six months in a cool cellar.

Pancetta: Like other Umbrian pork products, the pancetta of this region is exceptional. An unsmoked rolled bacon made from the belly of the animal, it is cured with salt, cloves, cinnamon or nutmeg, and pepper. Pancetta is used for larding meats or fish destined for the spit, the grill, or the oven. Above all, it is used to fortify flavors in a *battuto*, the Italian term for the mixture of chopped onion or garlic, carrot, celery, parsley, or other herb that is the aromatic foundation of many dishes. (As soon as it begins to sizzle in the sauté pan with olive oil, the *battuto* becomes a *soffritto*.) In yet another role, *pancetta* is a flavor foundation for the chopped mixture of onion or garlic and herbs that is used for flavoring or stuffing various dishes with the appellation *in porchetta*, meaning "in the manner of roasted suckling pig," a succulent treatment for particularly fortunate candidates from carp to chicken.

Prepared Meats

Galantine, *galantina* in Italian (derived from the Italian *gallina*, hen), is not unique to Umbrian cooking, but while other Italian cooks use only

Making Battuto

the royal barnyard bird, the capon, for making it, cooks in Perugia favor the chicken or guinea fowl. Because the chicken is a source of the egg, the dish is linked with the occasions of baptism, the wedding eve, and other special days that celebrate the cycle of life. For *galantina*, a large hen or guinea fowl is boned and stuffed with a mosaic of ground veal and pork, diced ham, veal tongue, mortadella, pistachios, *parmigiano-reggiano* cheese, and black truffles, the lot bound with egg and further enhanced with nutmeg and a judicious shot of dry *vin santo* or Marsala. The bird is then carefully stitched closed and immersed in broth to poach gently. After cooking and thorough chilling, the *galantina* is thinly sliced and served either as an antipasto or for a cold light lunch or dinner. It was once usual to hire women who were expert in making galantine to come into the home to prepare them for special occasions, rather than to risk less-than-extraordinary results. This practice has all but been replaced with ordering these elaborate preparations from specialty butchers.

Fresh pork specialties include an interesting fresh sausage available in two types: sweet, or *mazzafegati dolci* (sweet killed livers), and savory, or *mazzafegati salati* (salted killed livers). The sweet version consists of minced pork livers combined with raisins, pine nuts, orange zest, sugar, salt, and pepper, all stuffed into a sausage casing and roasted over an open fire. The savory version calls for seasoning the liver with garlic, pepper, and coriander seed. It also contains pine nuts and sultanas, but the orange zest and sugar are left out. Both types are swabbed with extra-virgin oive oil and sautéed, or impaled on a spit with bay leaves alternating between each link and cooked over a wood fire.

Sanguinaccio, once called *miaccetto*, is blood sausage. It consists of the fresh blood of the slaughtered pig, white wine, orange zest, and spices. Its popularity has decreased in Umbria in the last thirty years, but it is still made.

Roba cotta—"cooked stuff"—is a hash of sorts made with pork and whatever pork parts are left over after butchering the meat for prosciutto and other delicacies. The recipe consists of boiling the meats with garlic, spices, and dill seed, and then finely mincing them and stuffing the lot into a casing. *Roba cotta* was once an economical and popular snack sold by vendors who hawked it up and down the streets of Umbrian towns.

Umbrians love *salmi*, a terrinelike preparation that puts to use precious game whose meat is prized but which doesn't yield much for all the effort of the hunter. Many game birds are too tough to eat when roasted, another reason for the popularity of *salmi*. The tasty if tough and sparse meat of pheasant, quail, thrushes, pigeons, and so on is made into a kind of terrine with a carrot, celery, and onion trinity at the foundation, as well as other ingredients such as capers and prosciutto. The meat of goose, hare, and other game is also used. *Salmi* are typically made at home by ambitious cooks who have a hunter in the household to provide the meat, but they can also be bought from specialty butchers.

Olive Oil   Making extra virgin olive oil has been a refined craft in Umbria virtually since the inception of the region's recorded history. Ancient Etruria was one of the first areas in Italy to cultivate olive trees. Umbria, which provided ancient Rome with much of its food, became a prime area for olives. In the past, only the wealthiest households owned sufficient land to be able to produce enough olive oil to use in every aspect of meal preparation. The poor relied on pork fat for many of their cooked dishes and reserved their olive oil for seasoning food at the table. The cultivation of the olive tree and the craft of making the oil was interrupted during the Dark Ages, but a tremendous resurgence of production occurred during the ninth and tenth centuries due to a great demand by the Church, which wanted it for its liturgy, and the significant population shift from rural areas to urban centers. With this change, olive oil became accessible and affordable to the masses.

There is a saying in Umbria that good olive oil is a product of its mother. The sunny but sheltered Umbrian valleys, rocky slopes with good drainage, hospitable soil, and gentle climate provide the perfect environment for olive cultivation. The craft of extracting and bottling olive oil and the know-how for storing it properly in order to protect its fragile properties are highly developed in this region. Such practices account not only for the splendid olive oils one finds marked with the new government-regulated DOG (*di origine garantita*) labels, which restrict the source of the olives, but also for those oils sold *vendita diretta* from cottage-industry producers. Umbrian experts claim that 80 percent of their oils are extra-virgin, the highest percentage of extra-virgins anywhere in Italy.

On a culinary level, the mystique of Tuscan and Ligurian *olio d'oliva* has dominated the American market for many years, but within Italy, Umbrian oils are highly regarded. Artisanally produced Umbrian oils are among the rarest in the world. They are generally recognizable by their greenish yellow color; their gentle, clear, and clean fruity flavor, which gives a sensation of "softness" to the palate; and the absence of "oiliness"; Umbrian *olio* doesn't stick to the mouth; it is fluid on the tongue.

Within Umbria, oils from the Trasimeno area, where a comparatively warm microclimate exists, are "sweet" relative to oils from, for example, Spoleto, where the more rugged landscape and harsher climate result in *olio* that is more *piccante* and has a more grassy flavor. Spello *olio* is considered to be one of the finest, because the rocky hillside soil permits good drainage. Consequently, the earth in which the olive trees grow cannot retain the impurities that remain behind after a rainfall.

Flavor, freshness, and nutritional attributes are drastically affected by bottling (bottles should be dark, not transparent), storage (bottles should be kept in a dark and cool place), capping (an opened bottle should be vacuum sealed and corked well to halt the introduction of oxygen until the next use), and age (the younger the better). Labels on oils exported from Italy must now show not only the DOG demarcation, but the date the oil was made as well. These measures are designed to enable consumers to discern quality olive oil.

A great deal of confusion exists about the different types of olive oil available. Extra-virgin describes oil that is released from the first pressing of the olives. Cold-pressed indicates that the oil has been squeezed from the olives by the pressure of a moving wheel, without the use of heat, as such exposure would ruin it. To qualify for this highest rank, the

. . . an Italian gentleman never eats salad when traveling in foreign countries, for his palate, used to the finest oil, revolts against the liquid fit only for the lubrication of machinery he so often is offered in Germany, England, and France.

—COL. NEWHAM DAVIS, *THE GOURMET'S GUIDE TO EUROPE*, LONDON, 1911

FACING PAGE:
Olive picking in Trevi

olives must have been pressed no later than twenty-four hours after picking. Extra-virgin olive oil has an agreeable aroma, a pleasant and marked flavor, a vibrant amber-to-green color, and low acidity. Virgin olive oil comes from olives that were pressed after the prime twenty-four-hour period from tree to press. As fermentation begins, the acidity level in the olives rises, resulting in an inferior-grade oil. There is little virgin oil around, but it does appear now and then in food specialty markets. Pure olive oil is a somewhat misleading term, as it is made from blending virgin oil and refined olive oil. It is not a suitable substitute when extra-virgin olive oil is indicated, for it does not contribute flavor and most of its nutrients have been stripped away. Bottles labeled light (or lite) olive oil contain oil that bears no resemblance to genuine olive oil.

Finally, the lowest grade of olive oil is pomace, a noncooking oil. It is extracted by a chemical agent from the pulp that remains after olives have been pressed for their oil. Pomace is used for lamp oil in Italy, not for eating.

In the end, only extra-virgin olive oil is used in Umbrian cooking, whether one is deep-frying with it or drizzling it over a plate of sliced tomatoes.

Truffles The truffle, or *tartufo*, is a fungus that grows under the surface of calcareous soil with high clay content in symbiosis with particular tree roots. When the truffle organism finds the right conditions, it draws chlorophyll (it contains none of its own) and lymph from the host tree and inherits its color, scent, and flavor. The shape of the truffle depends on the soil in which it grows. Round, smooth-skinned truffles grow in soft earth. Truffles that grow in compact earth, which constrains their growth, are lumpy and gnarled. Truffles that grow in earth of varying density are somewhat squat and are colloquially called *piattella* or *piattina* (because they are platelike).

Since Roman times, black truffles have been sought after in the lush thickets and undergrowth of the Umbrian forests, where the rich soil provides the perfect environment for the fungus to grow. Truffles seem to have disappeared during the Middle Ages, along with other delights for the flesh, but they made their comeback during the Renaissance. They have been an important ingredient in Umbrian cuisine ever since.

Some ten truffle species are present in Umbria, but *Tuber melanosporum Vittadini*, comparable to the famous Périgord truffle, is the most precious due to its pungency and delicate aroma. Its skin is crinkled, and its interior is a deep brown violet-black when fully ripe. Fine cream-colored "veins" run through it, although they turn dark when the truffle is cooked. The black truffle lives symbiotically with the roots of common oak, holm oak, walnut, and a handful of other trees, and reaches full maturity from November to mid-March.

Black truffles need only a gentle rinsing to remove any clinging earth and should be dried with a soft cotton cloth. They should never be grated or chopped. Rather, they need to be crushed for maximum flavor. This is best accomplished with a mortar and pestle and a little salt and extra-virgin olive oil. Black truffles are often pounded into a paste with good olive oil for smearing on toast (*bruschetta*), or put into the cavity or on the surface of trout baked in parchment, where they can slowly release their flavor in the protection of the wrapping as the fish cooks. Truffles can also be added to game-bird stuffings, or stirred into the natural juices of the cooked bird for a splendid sauce.

There is a vast repertoire of Umbrian pasta sauces to which the black truffle adds its unique, beguiling flavor. These include fresh artichoke sauces, truffle butters, and mushroom sauces without tomato. The simplest sauce consists of warmed garlic-flavored extra-virgin olive oil into which pounded truffles are stirred before tossing with the cooked pasta.

The more highly prized white truffle, *Tuber magnatum pico*, has always been associated with magnificent dining on imperial tables where price was no object. It is also found in Piedmont, Tuscany, and in France. In Umbria, it prefers the conditions of the upper Tiber Valley, Orvieto, and the Gubbio-Gualdo zones, and is less abundant than the black truffle. Its favorite host plants are tall trees—the poplar, the linden, and the willow—although it also burrows in with the roots of the oak, the turkey

The truffle was born from the union of rain and lightning.

—THEOPHRASTUS, 372–287 B.C., IN *Work of Botany*

Norcia's Annual Truffle Festival

It is a piercing cold afternoon in Norcia. At makeshift stalls, vendors are hawking everything from home-made *limoncello* to artisanal boar salami, but the entire reason-for-being of this February festival is the local truffle "harvest." The truffle stalls are managed by the truffle finders, and one can get drunk on their bounty without spending a penny. "Taste this," all the vendors cry out. *Crema di tartufi*, or straight chopped truffles? Maybe a little white truffle butter on *bruschetta?* It is a food to which I can never say no.

Urbani, Umbria's largest exporter of this "black gold," overshadows the small truffle vendors, although the various truffle-paste samplings from the "little people" are also glorious and unforgettable. The Urbani "stand" is a two-storied building, and it boasts a truffle dipped in gold on display among piles of black ones. There are truffle pastes, truffle oils, fresh truffles, truffle everything for sale. Truffle buyers speaking halting Italian with all kinds of foreign accents are making deals with the Urbani men. Olga Urbani, heiress and empress, stands out like the aforementioned gold-dipped truffle amid the black ones. Turned out in a red fox fur coat and fur boots, she radiates the glamour of the prized fungus. She introduces me to Luigi Ciciriello, an Apulia-born restaurateur, bon vivant, and chef extraordinaire who owns a famous restaurant in Brussels, La Truffe Noire (The Black Truffle). The restaurant serves truffles only, which Ciciriello comes to Norcia to buy. "Fast-food truffles," he says, "I've made an art out of it."

Nearby, the truffle emperor, *papà* Carlo Urbani, is hosting a group of important-looking Germans in suits, who I soon discover are the largest importers of caviar in the world. Television cameramen begin to swarm the Urbani truffle pavilion, and Carlo Urbani is suddenly being broadcast on national television. "Caviar is not the ultimate aphrodisiac—truffles are," he quips to the interviewer. I accept an invitation to the truffle banquet the Urbani company is throwing for truffle buyers and guests in the evening at Grotta Azzurra, the oldest hotel in town.

There are hundreds of guests at the dinner. Elegantly dressed waiters balancing shiny platters of truffle-this and truffle-that above their heads weave their way through the standing guests, dispensing their antipasti. Truffles on *crostini*, truffles in flaky pastry, truffle mousse. I am seated with Olga on my right, and Luigi Ciciriello is across the table. Right behind me, at a parallel fifty-foot table, sit Carlo Urbani and the caviar men. The courses begin to arrive, starting with *tagliatelle* and white truffle cream. Veal with truffle sauce follows. Ciciriello frowns. "They don't know how to do it," he says. "Truffles are destroyed when they are grated. They have to be shaved." No matter, however, for behind me, I see Carlo Urbani working his magic, or the truffles are. A deal is struck.

The crowd of guests finally begins to disperse, everyone emptying into the little town. It is Sunday, but the doors of the bank directly across from the Grotta Azzurra are unlocked for Carlo Urbani and the Germans in suits. Television cameras appear again, poised to shoot the truffle emperor as he emerges from the shiny brass doors of the Banca di Spoleto. "Well," the television interviewer asked him, "is it true that caviar is the ultimate aphrodisiac?" "No," Urbani quips again, this time with a broader smile, "truffles are!"

—Norcia, 1998

oak, and the horn beam. The greatest specimens of the white truffle, those with great perfume, superior flavor, and rare delicacy, have an affinity with the tall tree species that grow along deep and shaded hillside ravines and wooded riverbanks. They ripen from October to December, but can be found in small numbers up to January if the winters are mild. The white truffle is recognized by its smooth, cream-colored or yellowish skin. Its interior is a clear brown that is sometimes blushed, and its veining is fine and clear, although it disappears when the truffle is cooked.

White truffles are handled differently than black ones. They are cleaned in the same manner, but they should be shaved into paper-thin flakes with a special handheld wooden device into which a razor is secured. They should never be cooked. Instead, they should be gently heated by scattering them over hot, uncomplicated dishes upon serving. In this way, their intricate perfume is slowly released and their flavor is intensified without being destroyed through intense heat. Foods that go best with white truffle are, in my opinion, eggs lightly scrambled in butter, fresh pasta with an uncomplicated butter-based sauce, *risotto in bianco* (rice cooked in butter with fresh veal and chicken broth, with *parmigiano-reggiano* cheese folded in at the end), trout cooked in butter (its flesh is naturally delicate and a perfect canvas for the light strokes of the truffle), and butter-sautéed tender veal scallopini deglazed with a little dry white wine. The white truffle shouldn't be added to dishes that contain garlic, vinegar, rustic tomato sauces, sheep's cheese, or other assertive ingredients.

One should beware of truffle essence that is artificially produced, mixed with olive oil, and passed off as the real thing. To prevent such fraud in restaurants, Remo Rossi of the Umbrian Gastronomical Association suggests insisting that the truffle be sliced directly onto the plate at the table.

Tuber aestivum, colloquially called *scorzone* or *bianchetto*, is a summer truffle that is abundant from June to October. Its skin is black, while its interior is creamy yellow to bronze with clear veining that lasts only until the truffle is cooked. This variety is found with oaks and pines. It is not as aromatic or flavorful as black or white truffles, and it combines well with other foods, including infusions with olive oil; in cream sauces for pasta; with mushrooms, butter, or creamy fresh cheese spreads for topping *crostini*; and in pâtés and cheeses. The summer truffle is cleaned with a stiff, damp brush to remove the dirt and a paring knife for cutting out any blemishes.

All fresh truffles should be stored in the same manner. The fresh truffle is a living thing. In order for its flavor and aroma to remain intact, it must be kept alive. Putting it in a jar of rice, a common suggestion, is a mistake. In that environment, it dies and dries out, losing its flavor and heady perfume. Instead, to store truffles for a few days, wrap them in dry butcher paper and then again in a layer of damp paper, followed by a second piece of dry paper. Keep them in the least chilly part of the refrigerator, or, if the weather is cool, leave them on a windowsill. Wherever the truffle is kept, its pungent aroma will remind you of its presence. In recent years, methods for freezing truffles with particular precautions have proven successful. The fresh truffles must first be vacuum sealed, then immediately stored in a freezer. With careful storage, truffles can keep their organoleptic properties for two years or more.

FACING PAGE:
Black truffles

Breads

pane

1

You smell like the loaves of hot bread just out of the oven that the farm wife brings into the big farm kitchen.

—Furio Miselli, poet, Terni

Bread styles mark Italian regions as much as pasta varieties or types of sweets do. For this reason, and because bread is not easily combined with anything else, some of the breads that are unique to Umbria have been given their own chapter. Many more breads particular to Umbria exist, of course, but this small collection draws from around the region and represents different places in the meal and different seasons of the year. Umbrian bakeries make a wide range of superb regional breads daily, so that baking one's own bread is hardly necessary. The recipes here are for uncomplicated breads that are more typically produced in the home kitchen.

In the past, bread was made once a week by the housewife, a task that began at sunrise, and the loaves were baked in the village or town communal oven. A small part of the dough was always set aside as leavening for the following week's loaves. The process of making the dough, allowing it to ferment, and transforming it into loaves is as feminine a ritual as birth. In a region as steeped in mysticism as Umbria, the ritual is also imbued with spiritual significance. Guglielma Corsi's classic *Un secolo di cucina umbra* instructs, ". . . pound the dough well with your hand and then cover it with a layer of flour. Trace on it with one finger two lines in the form of a cross; this helps the bread to rise and at the same time it is a gesture in honor of God." Others follow the gesture of tracing the cross into the bread with a prayer, repeating three times, "Father, Son, Holy Spirit." The cross on the loaf faces upward, toward heaven. This ritual is still practiced today in Umbria, particularly in areas where grain is grown.

The region's traditional table bread is saltless, due to the heavy taxes on salt levied by the Catholic church until it lost its dominions upon unification in 1861. To this day, saltless bread remains a symbol of a proud and fierce population whose spirit was never broken by the hated clerics and their armies who set up residence throughout the land in order to carry out their oppressive laws. Saltless bread is meant to be eaten with prosciutto, which in both Umbria and Tuscany is salted, thus bypassing the need to salt twice. Omitting the salt permits the flavor of the wheat and the flavor of the foods to be appreciated.

According to local wisdom, bread was always eaten fresh on the first day. On the second, it was used for *bruschetta*. On the third day, when it was neither too soft nor too hard, it was perfect for *panzanella*, the bread salad that is widespread throughout central Italy. The Umbrian version of the salad, which long predates the acceptance of the tomato in Italy, is made with three-day-old bread, fresh basil, extra-virgin olive oil, and wine vinegar. Thus, hard bread was used for many things, such as to add substance to soups, as in the Tuscan *ribollita* or *pappa col pomodoro*, but also in many Umbrian soups.

The quintessential Umbrian bread is no doubt *torta al testo*, sometimes called *torta sul testo*. In Gubbio and Città di Castello, it is called *panaro*. *Torta al testo* is a quick, very thin, flat, round griddle bread rooted in antiquity. It is used as a table bread or as a wrap for fillings. Prior to modern times, when most households had no ovens and most cooking was done on the stove top, such griddle breads were common. The most commonplace fillings are savory, among them hard-cooked eggs, cheese, prosciutto or other cured meats, boiled broccoli rabe or greens sautéed with olive oil and garlic, grilled sausages or a combination of sausages and greens, greens with sautéed potatoes or beans, or slices of roasted meats.

Umbrian holidays have their own representative breads. Sweet breads are usually associated with particular saint days and other celebratory days. *Torcolo di San Costanzo*, named after the benefactor of Perugia, is one of these. The origin of the ring-shaped pastry is ancient. *Torcoli*, "ring shapes," are female fertility symbols. The *sagra del torcolo*, a festival that goes back to Etruscan times, is based on the ceremonial eating of a pastry *torcolo*. Until fairly recently, in the small mountain city of Nocera Umbra, an annual grand ball was held at which it was customary for the girls to bring baskets of pastry *torcoli*. If a girl found a boy to her liking, she would remove a *torcolo* from the basket and place it on his head. The gesture was symbolic of mating. Similar customs of crowning the heads of unattached young men with pastry rings appear in other Umbrian traditions.

Master Bread

pane

makes 2 loaves

$^1/_2$ cup warm water (100 to 110°F)

1 cake (20 grams) fresh yeast, or 1 envelope ($2^1/_2$ teaspoons) active dry yeast

about 4 cups unbleached bread flour

1 teaspoon sea salt

1 cup cold water

1 tablespoon extra-virgin olive oil, plus oil for oiling dough, bowl, and pans

fine cornmeal or semolina for dusting

In Umbria today, bread is made both with and without salt. This is a recipe for salted bread dough, and it is the basis of three other recipes in the chapter. A small bowl filled with water set on the floor of the oven makes it unnecessary to spray the loaves continually during baking to achieve a nicely colored crust.

Place ¼ cup of the warm water in a medium bowl. Crumble in the fresh yeast or sprinkle in the dry yeast. Stir and let stand in a warm place until foamy, about 10 minutes.

In a large, shallow bowl, sift 1 cup of the flour with the salt. Make a well in the center. Add the remaining ¼ cup warm water, the cold water, and the 1 tablespoon olive oil to the yeast mixture and stir gently. Pour the mixture into the well. Using a wooden spoon, gradually stir the flour into the liquid until it is absorbed. Gradually sift in 2 more cups of the flour. When the dough becomes stiff, use your hands to form the dough into a ball.

Lightly sprinkle flour on a work surface. Place the ball of dough on the floured surface and knead it while gradually sifting onto it as much of the remaining 1 cup flour as needed to form a dough that is silky and elastic, 8 to 10 minutes. Shape into a ball.

To make the dough in a food processor, place ¼ cup of the warm water in a medium bowl. Crumble in the fresh yeast or sprinkle in the dry yeast. Stir and let stand in a warm place until foamy, about 10 minutes. Meanwhile, in the bowl of a food processor, combine 3¾ cups of the flour and the salt, and pulse to mix, about 30 seconds. Add the

BREADS

remaining ¼ cup warm water, the cold water, and the 1 tablespoon olive oil to the yeast mixture. Stir gently and pour into the processor with the flour and salt. Engage the processor until a ball has formed, about 40 seconds. It will still be somewhat sticky at this point. Transfer the dough to a lightly floured board and knead until silky and elastic, 3 to 4 minutes, adding more flour as necessary to achieve the proper consistency. Shape into a ball.

Place the dough in a larger, clean, lightly oiled bowl. Lightly brush the surface of the dough with olive oil. Stretch plastic wrap tightly across the bowl, covering it completely, then cover the plastic wrap with a kitchen towel. Allow the dough to rise undisturbed at room temperature in a location free of drafts until doubled in bulk, 4 to 5 hours (the longer the rise, the lighter the dough). If the dough rises too quickly, punch it down and let it rise again.

If baking the loaves on baking stones or terra-cotta tiles, sprinkle a baker's peel with cornmeal. If you have baking stones or tiles but no peel, dust a large, rimless baking sheet with cornmeal and use it for transferring the loaves to the stones or tiles. If you are not using stones or tiles, brush a large baking sheet with olive oil and sprinkle with cornmeal or semolina.

Punch down the dough in the bowl and turn it out onto a lightly floured work surface. Knead it for several minutes until it is once again elastic. Divide

the dough in half and form each half into a round loaf. Place the loaves on the cornmeal- or semolina-dusted peel or baking sheet or on the oiled baking sheet. Sprinkle the tops of the loaves with bread flour, then cover with a kitchen towel. Let rise in a warm, draft-free spot until doubled in bulk, about 2 hours, or in a cool, draft-free spot overnight.

If using baking stones or terra-cotta tiles, place them on the middle rack of the oven and begin preheating the oven to 400 degrees F 40 minutes before baking, to ensure the baking surfaces are hot. If not using stones or tiles, begin preheating the oven at least 20 minutes before baking.

Place a small, shallow pan of water on the bottom of the oven. Remove the towel from the loaves. If using a baking stone or tiles, slide the loaves off the peel (or the baking sheet) directly onto the heated surface. If using a baking pan, slide it onto the middle rack. Bake the loaves until golden and cooked through, about 30 minutes. The test for doneness is to rap the loaves on the bottom. If they sound hollow, they are done. Transfer to racks to cool for at least 15 minutes before cutting.

Griddle Bread

torta al testo

makes six 6-inch flatbreads

2¼ cups unbleached bread flour, plus more as needed

½ teaspoon baking soda

½ teaspoon sea salt

1 cup warm water or milk (100 to 110°F), or as needed

In the past, the traditional cooking surface for this simple flat bread was a smooth, fireproof stone called la schiaccia, *which was kept in the center of the hearth, always hot and ready. Today, this stone has been replaced with* il testo, *a slab made from a mixture of crushed common stones, marble chips, and concrete, or a thick, round griddle pan with knob handles for use on the stove top. Outside of Umbria,* torta al testo *can be made on a piece of one-inch-thick soapstone placed over a gas burner. Failing that, a well-seasoned cast-iron skillet will suffice.*

At one time, the bread was made of nothing more than flour and water. Nowadays, a pinch of baking soda is added for leavening. Using warm liquid makes the dough more pliable, and thus easier to stretch out into a thin disk. Adding milk instead of water results in a more tender dough.

Torta al testo is eaten as any other plain table bread. It is almost always present with pollo arrabbiata *(page 93) and other dishes where there are plenty of pan juices for dipping.*

In a bowl, mix together the 2¼ cups flour, baking soda, and salt. Add the liquid and mix well, first with a wooden spoon, then with your hands, to form a ball of dough. The dough should be soft and pliable but firm—as soft to the touch as a baby's bottom. Alternatively, combine all the ingredients in a food processor. Pulse to form a soft, uniform ball of dough.

Divide the dough into 6 equal portions and form each portion into a ball. Cover the balls with kitchen towels and let them rest for 15 to 30 minutes. This will permit the dough to relax.

Working with 1 ball at a time, flatten it into a disk and place on a floured work surface. Using a rolling pin, then your hands to stretch it more, roll each dough ball into the same shape as the *testo* or other cooking surface. The dough should be about ⅛ inch thin. Puncture it with the prongs of a fork.

Heat the *testo* or other cooking surface over high heat. Toss a little flour on the surface; when the flour colors, the surface is ready. Transfer a dough round to the hot surface and cook, turning once, until nicely colored but not too dark on both sides, about 4 minutes total. Serve each round the moment it comes off the heat, as it will harden quickly.

How to Cook Pizzas at Home

In the 1800s, families lacked ovens, so various types of flat breads were cooked on the schiacce. This was a roughly polished slab of stone, three centimeters [a generous inch] thick and of various sizes. Our grandmothers kept them in a permanently vertical position in the central part of the inner fireplace wall. Thus, every time they lit the fire, the stone was heated, making it always ready for cooking pizzas. Today the schiaccia has been replaced by the testo, which is made by combining small marble chips, collected from the sides of ditches, and concrete. The chips are crushed, mixed with the concrete, and then pressed into specially designed molds. When dry and hard, the forms are turned out of the molds and fired in brick ovens. The testo can be heated over hot embers or a gas flame. The right moment for cooking pizza is when the testo has taken on a white cast. If you want to cook the pizza over embers [charcoal that isn't smoldering], position the testo atop a tripod [an iron triangle with three legs attached], an indispensable tool that supports a cooking surface over the embers without smothering the fire.

Guglielma Corsi,
—*Un secolo di cucina umbra*

Pecorino Cheese Rings in the Style of Todi

ciambelle al formaggio

makes about eight 4-inch rings

Master Bread dough (page 34)

$1/4$ pound semisoft pecorino cheese
(see recipe introduction), half grated and half
coarsely chopped

3 tablespoons extra-virgin olive oil, plus extra
oil for oiling pan

*This cheese bread and many versions of it are
traditional for Easter breakfast and for Epiphany
on January 6. Sometimes called* torcoletti, *the
recipe for these traditional savory buns calls for
pecorino cheese from Todi (see Cheeses, page 13).
But such sheep's milk cheeses are rarely stocked
even by the most knowledgeable and well-stocked
cheese purveyors outside of Umbria, so a semisoft
Sardinian or Tuscan sheep's milk cheese may
be used in its place. Some modern versions of the
rings include eggs in the dough, which produce
a sweeter, puffier result.*

Prepare the dough as directed in the master recipe. After
it has risen the second time, punch it down and work in
the grated and chopped cheese and the 3 tablespoons olive
oil, kneading vigorously to make a uniform mixture.

Generously oil a large baking sheet with olive oil. Divide
the dough into 8 equal portions. On a floured surface,
use your hands to roll each portion back and forth into a
rope about 8 inches long. Form each rope into a ring
and pinch the ends together to secure. Place the rings on
the prepared baking sheet, then flip them over to coat
both sides with oil. Cover the pan with a kitchen towel and
place the pan in a warm, draft-free spot until the rings
double in bulk, about 1 hour. Meanwhile, preheat an oven
to 400 degrees F.

Slide the pan onto the middle rack of the oven and bake
until golden, about 15 minutes. To determine doneness,
tap the underside of the rings; they should emit a hollow
sound. Transfer the rings to a rack and allow to rest for
at least 10 to 15 minutes. Eat warm or cool.

*When I was growing up on my parents' farm, I watched the peasants
make special foods for the holy days. One of their breads was*
ciambelle al formaggio, *made of yeast dough to which they added
the sheep's milk cheese they also crafted. These* ciambelle *were
eaten for breakfast only on holy days. On Easter, they made another
kind of cheese bread,* torta, *with norcino and romanesco cheeses.
All of these special foods were always brought to the local church
for a blessing by the priest before they were eaten.*

—DONATELLA PLATONI, SOLOMEO

Flat Bread with Sage and Onions

schiacciata con la salvia e la cipolla

for 6 to 8 people as an antipasto or snack

Master Bread dough (page 34)

6 small or 4 medium-sized onions, quartered and then finely sliced

sea salt

$^{1}/_{2}$ cup extra-virgin olive oil, plus oil for oiling pan, if using

16 large fresh sage leaves, or 3 tablespoons crumbled dried sage

Cornmeal or semolina for sprinkling

What Umbrians call schiacciata is sometimes known as focaccia in other parts of Italy. The word schiacciata comes from the verb schiacciare, "to crush" or "to flatten." While flat bread with an onion topping is found elsewhere in Italy, this Umbrian version is somewhat unusual in that the onions are salted prior to being lightly fried and placed on the bread. The salt forces liquid out, resulting in a lighter, less soggy topping.

This flat bread is found throughout Umbria and, as usual, many variations exist. In Città di Castello, in the northwest, it is called pampassato. *There, rosemary sometimes replaces sage. In Norcia, where the pig reigns, the bread is called* spianata, *and* ciccioli, *thinly sliced pork cracklings, are sometimes strewn on the surface. Other variations include substituting zucchini or cooked potato slices for the onion, both of which are also salted before cooking.*

Prepare the dough as directed in the master recipe. While it is rising the second time, prepare the topping: Place the sliced onions in a colander, sprinkle lightly with salt, and let stand for 1 hour. Then, gather the onions in your hands and squeeze them fairly tightly. A great deal of liquid will be released as a result of the salt interacting with the onions.

In a skillet, warm the ½ cup olive oil over medium heat. When it is hot enough to make the onions sizzle, add the onions and sauté until they are softened, 6 to 7 minutes. Toss in the sage at this point, stir, and then remove the onions from the heat.

If you will be baking the flat bread on a baking sheet, brush a baking sheet with olive oil and sprinkle lightly

continued

39

Flat Bread with Sage and Onions
continued

with cornmeal or semolina. If you will be using a baking stone or terra-cotta tiles, sprinkle a baker's peel generously with cornmeal or semolina. If you have a baking stone or tiles but no peel, dust a large, rimless baking sheet generously with cornmeal or semolina and use it for transferring the flat bread to the stone or tiles.

When the dough has completed its second rising, punch it down in the bowl and turn it out onto a lightly floured work surface. Knead it for several minutes until it is once again elastic, then stretch and shape it to fill the oiled baking sheet. It should be no more than ½ inch thick. Spread the onion mixture evenly over the surface of the dough. If using a baking stone or tiles, shape the dough on the prepared baker's peel or baking sheet, again making it no more than ½ inch thick, and top with the onion mixture. Drape the baking sheet or peel with a sheet of plastic wrap, then cover with a kitchen towel. Let rise in a warm, draft-free spot until doubled in bulk, about 1 hour. (Adding the topping before the final rising permits the flavor of the onion to permeate the dough.)

If using a baking stone or terra-cotta tiles, place on the middle rack of the oven and begin preheating the oven to 400 degrees F 40 minutes before baking, to ensure the baking surface is hot. If not using a stone or tiles, begin preheating the oven at least 20 minutes before baking.

When the third rise is completed, remove the towel and plastic wrap and slide the baking sheet onto the middle rack of the oven, disturbing the risen volume of the dough as little as possible. If using a stone or tiles, carefully slide the rectangle off the peel (or the baking sheet) directly onto the heated surface, again disturbing the risen volume as little as possible. Bake until cooked through but neither too hard nor too brown, about 20 to 30 minutes. Transfer the flat bread to a rack and let it settle for 10 to 15 minutes. Cut into squares and serve hot or warm.

Saint Costanzo's Sweet Yeast Bread with Anise and Candied Orange Peel

torcolo di San Costanzo

makes 1 large ring

3/4 cup tepid water

1 envelope (2 1/2 teaspoons) active dry yeast, or 1 cake (20 grams) fresh yeast

1/2 cup sugar

3 tablespoons melted or softened unsalted butter, plus butter for greasing pan and brushing over the bread

3 tablespoons extra-virgin olive oil

2 1/2 cups bread flour

1/4 teaspoon salt

1 tablespoon orange flower water, if available, or substitute 2 teaspoons orange zest

1 teaspoon anise seeds, or to taste

1/3 cup (3 ounces) candied orange peel, chopped

1/3 cup (2 ounces) pine nuts

1/3 cup sultanas

milk for brushing the bread

Saint Costanzo, for whom this specialty is named, is the patron saint of Perugia. The sweet bread is baked in a ring mold. Torcolo di San Costanzo is eaten with vin santo *(sweet wine), or with espresso.*

In a large mixing bowl, combine the 3/4 cup of tepid water and the yeast. Let it stand until it foams, about 6 minutes. Add 1 tablespoon of the sugar; if the yeast is active, the mixture should double. To the yeast mixture in the bowl, add the butter, olive oil, remaining sugar, flour, salt, and orange flower water or orange zest, and the aniseeds.

Beat at low speed with an electric mixer with a dough hook attachment, for 2 minutes, scraping down the bowl occasionally. Beat at high speed for 3 minutes. If mixing by hand, knead for at least 15 minutes. A uniform, elastic dough should result. Cover the bowl with plastic wrap, then several layers of kitchen towels, and set it in a warm, draft-free place until doubled in bulk, about 3 hours.

Butter an oven-proof ring mold. When the dough has risen, turn it out onto a board. Add the candied peel, the pine nuts, and the sultanas and knead well to incorporate, until the dough is smooth and elastic, adding flour as necessary if the dough is sticky. Shape the dough into a rope long enough to form a ring in the ring mold. Pinch the ends together. Put the dough in the ring mold. Brush the top with melted butter. Cover with plastic wrap and then a kitchen towel, place in a warm spot, and let the dough rise again until doubled in bulk, about 3 hours.

Preheat an oven to 375 degrees F. Uncover the pan and brush the top of the dough with milk. Re-cover with fresh plastic wrap, and then a towel, and let rest for 10 minutes. Bake on the middle rack until well risen and golden and a cake tester inserted into the bread comes out clean, about 25 minutes. Transfer to a rack and let cool before serving.

BREADS

Appetizers, Snacks, and Condiments

antipasti, merende, e salsette

2

Appetizers are teasers. At the beginning of the meal, they seduce the eaters—as the Italians say, "grab them by the throat"—convincing them to stay for dinner. But they may also tease between the courses, appearing in their role as *intermezzi*. An appetizer may even comprise the whole meal, either served alone in a sizable portion or in commune with other antipasti. Sometimes appetizers are nowhere near the meal, instead masquerading as snacks *(merende)* for the impatient before Italy's lunch bells begin to ring at one o'clock. Likewise, they can lure the worker on the way home to dinner off the prescribed path.

The wide range of exceptional *salumi*, cured meat specialties, are among the most typical of all the antipasti. The pantry section (page 13) describes in detail some of the numerous high-quality *salumi* found in Umbria.

Crostini and *bruschetta* crowned with countless delicious toppings are particularly popular antipasti as well, and a few of them are included here. Truffles naturally find their way to the appetizer course, and so do the many wild mushrooms of the region. Many vegetable antipasti are constructed, too, among them tomatoes stuffed with seasoned rice; black olives marinated in extra-virgin olive oil, garlic, bay leaves, and orange rind; and *torta al testo* filled with cooked greens or other stuffings (page 36).

Egg dishes appear in the roles of antipasto and *merenda*, too. I am convinced that Umbrians eat more eggs than anyone else in Italy, primarily because I have never seen such variety in frittatas as I have seen in Umbria. Mint frittata, garlic scape frittata, green fig frittata, escarole frittata, dandelion greens frittata, frittata of peas, of favas, of chard, of wild greens *(l'erbe)*, of wild asparagus, of wild hops—of nearly anything. Reading through an Umbrian cookbook of the seventeenth century, the frittata entries are proportionately even more numerous—and elegant— than they are today: spinach frittata with almond sauce; frittata, hunter's style, with Persian rose water sauce; country-style frittata with a *coulis* of peas; onion frittata with milk sauce; sweetbread frittata with a *coulis* of meat; eggplant frittata with frog sauce; beet frittata with rose water sauce.

When I was a girl, the contadini *ate large breakfasts usually consisting of frittata before they went to the fields. They even drank wine in the morning. Now we eat frittata for a little snack.*

—Donatella Platoni, Solomeo

With all the fantasia that goes and has gone into the frittata, it is interesting to note that Umbrians don't typically mix grated hard aged cheese into the egg mixture, a departure from the way the frittata is usually made elsewhere. Other *piatti di uova*, "egg dishes," turn up, too, including many variations of *uova in camicia*, "in a shirt," that is, sauced. The sauce might be made of tomatoes or asparagus. But the best egg dish of all is scrambled eggs with sweet Umbrian butter and freshly shaved white truffles—and no sauce at all.

The word *salse*, or "sauces," is from the Latin word for salt. Like salt, sauce is something that embellishes, that delivers a marked flavor. So if salt and pepper are periods, a sauce is an exclamation point. Sauces are few and far between on the Umbrian table, except for those that are devised for pasta, are created as a vehicle for black or white truffles, or are put together to moisten roasts as they cook slowly *allo spiedo*, "on the spit." The fresh, pure, natural foods upon which Umbrian cooking is based are brimming with their inherent flavors and need no saucing. What sauces do exist in the cook's repertoire are teasers, bringing out what is already there, and thus playing a role not unlike that played by antipasti.

Black Truffles on Toast

crostini alla Urbani

for 4 people

2 ounces black truffles, fresh or conserved

$1/4$ teaspoon sea salt

5 tablespoons extra-virgin olive oil

freshly ground black pepper

1 very small clove garlic, finely minced

$1/4$ teaspoon fresh lemon juice

$1/4$ teaspoon high-quality white or red wine vinegar

8 to 10 small, thin slices coarse country bread

⇒ *This recipe comes from the Urbani family, Umbria's most prominent truffle merchants. The olive oil must be of the highest quality, and so, too, must the bread, which should also be freshly sliced and, preferably, toasted over an open fire. The simplest recipes, such as this one, get at the truffle's clear flavor and aroma.*

If using fresh truffles, rinse gently and dry with a soft cloth. Put the fresh or conserved truffles in a good-sized mortar. Pound them to a fine consistency with the salt, drizzling in 3 tablespoons of the olive oil at the same time.

In a small skillet, gently warm the remaining 2 tablespoons olive oil and add the pounded truffles. Add pepper to taste and heat the truffles gently in the oil.

Meanwhile, combine the garlic, lemon juice, and vinegar in a small, sturdy crock or a small mortar and pound the garlic to smash it as much as possible. Add it to the truffles and warm all together over low heat for a minute or so, enough to allow the flavors to be released. Remove the truffles from the heat. Check for salt.

Toast the bread slices lightly. While still warm, spread with the truffle paste. Serve immediately.

Crostini with Chicken Liver Paste

crostini di fegatini di pollo

for 4 to 6 people

5 tablespoons extra-virgin olive oil, plus oil for drizzling

1 onion, minced

1 pound chicken gizzards, trimmed of tough outer membranes and coarsely chopped

1 pound chicken liver, trimmed of any dark spots, fat, and membranes, then quartered

2 tablespoons dry white wine

12 juniper berries, crushed

1 tablespoon minced fresh sage, or 1 teaspoon crumbled dried sage

$1/2$ teaspoon sea salt, or to taste

freshly ground black pepper

coarse country bread, 8 to 12 small, thin slices

In an ample skillet, warm the 5 tablespoons olive oil over medium-low heat. Add the onion and sauté until nicely softened but not browned, 5 to 7 minutes. Add the gizzards and livers and continue to sauté to color them nicely, about 10 minutes. Take care not to overcook them. Now add the wine and allow the alcohol and the excess liquid released from the livers to evaporate, about 5 minutes. Add the juniper berries, sage, salt, and a generous amount of pepper and remove from the heat.

When the mixture has cooled slightly, transfer it to a food processor or a blender and grind to form a uniform mixture, but do not grind to a smooth paste. The finished spread should still have some of the texture of the gizzards.

Toast the bread slices lightly. Spread the paste on them. If you are using a high-quality olive oil, drizzle a little oil over the spread. Serve warm or at room temperature.

APPETIZERS, SNACKS, AND CONDIMENTS

≫ *Chicken livers are combined with gizzards in this rustic Umbrian pâté that resembles the better-known Tuscan chicken liver topping for* crostini. *After grinding them, the livers are fairly smooth, while the gizzards retain their coarser texture, making the mixture quite different from a liver-only spread. Duck or goose livers and gizzards are also used in the same proportions. This type of liver paste is always served on small rounds of toasted bread.*

Prenuptial Meat Patties

polpettini di carne prenuziali

for 8 people

1 cup cubed stale white bread, crusts removed (about 2 ounces with crust)

$^1/_2$ cup milk or meat or vegetable broth

1 pound mixed ground pork and veal, in equal amounts, ground twice

$^1/_2$ pound ground chicken breast

2 ounces prosciutto, coarsely chopped

1 small onion, grated on the large oval holes of a box grater

2 teaspoons chopped fresh marjoram, or 1 teaspoon crumbled dried marjoram

grated zest of $^1/_2$ small lemon

1 egg, lightly beaten

2 teaspoons sea salt, plus salt to taste

freshly ground black pepper

olive oil or corn oil for frying

unbleached flour for dredging

In Umbria it was once, and still is in some homes, a ritual for a mother-in-law-to-be to prepare these meat patties the day before the wedding of her son. Upon entering her new husband's family home, the bride-to-be would be offered the platter of patties cooked in tomato sauce. The mother-in-law would bid her to take one, saying, "Daughter-in-law, may you be the joy of my home. Will you bring discord or union?" The bride, of course, is meant to answer, "Union." At that point the mother-in-law would respond, "Then eat your polpettina."

Polpettine are the diminutive of polpette, *"meatballs," although I find this common English translation an unsatisfactory one for these savory little delicacies. The patties are most often browned in oil, then transferred to a pot of tomato sauce to finish cooking. In summer, I like to cook them through by frying, drain them on paper towels, and then serve them impaled on a sturdy twig of fresh rosemary, which is always plentiful in my garden that time of year.*

Put the bread cubes in a small bowl and add the milk or broth. When the bread is softened thoroughly, squeeze it dry, discarding the liquid, and place the cubes in a bowl. Add the pork and veal, chicken, prosciutto, onion, marjoram, lemon zest, egg, and 2 teaspoons salt and season with pepper to taste. Using your hands, blend the mixture well. Scoop up 2 rounded teaspoons for each patty and form into an egg shape.

Pour the oil to a depth of $^1/_2$ inch into a large, wide skillet and place over medium heat. Meanwhile, lightly dredge in flour only as many patties as you will fry in the first batch. When the oil is hot enough to make the patties sizzle upon contact, slip them into the pan one at a time, being careful

continued

Prenuptial Meat Patties
continued

not to crowd the pan. Fry until nicely browned all over and cooked through, about 10 minutes.

Using tongs or a slotted spatula, transfer to paper towels to drain, then place on a platter and keep warm. Taste a patty for salt and, if necessary, sprinkle salt sparingly over the patties. Serve hot or warm.

Tomato Sauce Variation:
To prepare the meat patties in tomato sauce, prepare a double recipe of the sauce for Handmade Umbricelli with Quick Tomato Sauce (page 77). Make and cook the patties as directed, then simmer them together with the sauce for 10 minutes before serving.

Umbrian Sauce for Fish

salsa umbra

makes a generous ½ cup
for serving with 3 pounds of fish

> *The anchovies disappear into the sauce when mashed with the minced capers, and the resulting mix is a piquant foil to the delicate flesh of boiled or roasted freshwater or saltwater fish.*

¹/₂ cup high-quality extra-virgin olive oil

3 large cloves garlic, crushed

1 fresh rosemary sprig, about 6 inches long

8 anchovy fillets packed in olive oil, drained and chopped

5 tablespoons capers, minced

In a small saucepan, combine half of the olive oil with the garlic and rosemary and warm over low heat until the oil absorbs a good deal of the garlic essence and the garlic is well softened but has not colored, 10 to 12 minutes. Discard the garlic.

Transfer the oil to a small bowl and add the anchovies and capers. Mash the anchovies and capers into the oil. Stir in the remaining olive oil and serve as a table sauce.

APPETIZERS, SNACKS, AND CONDIMENTS

Guglielma Corsi's Roasted Peppers
with Anchovies, Mint, and Lemon

peperoni arrostiti alla Guglielma Corsi

for 4 people

4 red bell peppers

10 or 12 anchovy fillets packed in olive oil, drained

handful of fresh mint leaves

juice of $1/4$ small lemon

extra-virgin olive oil for drizzling

A few peppers remained from my summer crop and the mint was asserting itself through the bricks on the path some time after I noticed this recipe in Signora Corsi's book, Un' amica in cucina per voi giovani *(A Friend in the Kitchen for You Young People). Upon first reading, the flavor combination of peppers, anchovies, and mint had seemed strange to me, but having learned the extent to which herbs of many kinds are an integral part of Umbrian cooking and knowing Corsi's infallible palate, I remembered the recipe. The peppers and the mint beckoned to be picked before the frost, there was a tin of anchovies in my pantry, and I still had a small supply of olive oil I had brought back from that last olive pressing in Umbria. Lovely.*

To roast the peppers, arrange them on a baking sheet. Place the baking sheet 3 inches under a preheated broiler or in an oven preheated to 400 degrees F. Alternatively, place them on a grill rack above a charcoal fire. Roast them until they are charred all over and tender inside, turning them frequently to ensure that they blacken evenly, about 30 minutes in the oven but less time by the other methods. When the peppers are cool enough to handle, peel off the skins using your fingertips, cut the peppers in half lengthwise, and remove and discard the stems, ribs, and seeds. (Do not do this under running water; it will wash away some of the delicious smoky flavor.) For this dish, I like to slice each pepper section into 2 or 3 strips.

Arrange the pepper strips in an attractive circular fashion on a serving platter. Fit the whole anchovy fillets in between the pepper sections, making a pattern of several pepper strips alternating with an anchovy fillet, to present a pleasing design. Strew the mint leaves generously over the peppers, leaving them whole if they are small and tearing them into several pieces if they are large. Sprinkle the peppers lightly with the lemon juice, then drizzle lightly with the olive oil. Serve at room temperature.

Frittata with Fresh Garlic Scapes

frittata con l'aglietto fresco

for 4 to 6 people as an appetizer
or 2 people for lunch

6 eggs

³/₄ teaspoon sea salt

freshly ground black pepper

¹/₂ pound tender garlic scapes,
or 4 or 5 bunches scallions

¹/₄ cup extra-virgin olive oil

Garlic scapes are the tender green shoots of the garlic bulb that come up in spring weeks before the bulbs are mature enough to uproot. Garlic is worth growing in the garden. Freshly pulled, the bulbs are lighter, juicier, and more subtle than those sold in the markets. As for the tender shoots, my farmer friend, Black Soil Eddy, calls them scapes, and during the short period when they crop up, they should be snatched for their excellent flavor, which is particularly nice with eggs.

In Umbria, the scapes are sometimes used in frittatas, and as with all frittatas, the object is to form a mixture that contains as much filling as can be bound by the eggs, unlike the idea behind a French omelet. Four to five bunches of scallions can be substituted, although the flavor will be different.

In a bowl, lightly whisk together the eggs, salt, and a generous amount of pepper; set aside.

Wash the scapes well to remove any traces of dirt. Trim off any discolorations. If using scallions, trim off the root ends of the bulbs and cut off and discard all but 5 inches of the green tops and any discolored greens. Cut the scapes or scallions on the diagonal into ¹/₂-inch slices. Immerse them in a saucepan filled with boiling salted water and blanch for 1 minute. Drain well.

Preheat a broiler. In a 10- or 12-inch heavy-bottomed flameproof skillet or omelet pan, warm the olive oil over medium-high heat. Add the scapes or scallions and sauté them for about 2 minutes. Pour the beaten eggs into the pan and use the back of a wooden spoon to even out the mixture in the pan. Reduce the heat to medium-low and cook very gently on the bottom, moving the pan around on the surface of the burner to ensure even cooking. It is important that the heat not be too high, or the frittata will dry out on the bottom and remain raw in the center. When it is set and cooked on the bottom, after 5 to 7 minutes, remove it from the stove top. Slide the pan onto a rack about 9 inches from the broiler element. Leave the oven door ajar and remain with the frittata, watching over it until it is cooked through and golden on the surface, 5 to 7 minutes, depending upon the width of the pan. To test for doneness, press a finger in the center of the frittata to see if it is firm. If it is runny, slide it back onto the rack to continue cooking, always watching over it.

Remove the frittata from the broiler and let it cool somewhat, then carefully transfer it to a platter. Allow it to cool to room temperature before serving.

Frittata with Asparagus and Wild Herbs

frittata con asparagi e erbe selvatici

for 3 or 4 people

1 pound asparagus, preferably pencil-thin

sea salt for cooking asparagus,
plus 3/4 teaspoon, or to taste

5 eggs, lightly beaten

2 tablespoons chopped fresh mint

3 tablespoons chopped fresh fennel fronds

3 tablespoons extra-virgin olive oil

In the most popular Umbrian variety of this frittata, nothing is added to the eggs but the immensely flavorful asparagi di bosco, "forest asparagus," that grows wild in the countryside. In other variations, erbe selvatiche, "wild herbs," are added that might include young dandelion shoots, nettle tips, cresses, and hops. The flavor of the tender frond of the American fiddlehead fern is not unlike that of the wild asparagus of Umbria. When it is to be found, it may be substituted, giving it the same treatment of first poaching quickly before adding it to the beaten egg.

Trim off the tough ends of the asparagus. If the spears are not perfectly fresh and tender, beginning near the base of each spear, peel away the thicker skin to reveal the tender stalk underneath, stopping within a few inches of the tip.

In a large skillet, boil enough water to cover the asparagus. Add salt (1 teaspoon per quart water) and lower the asparagus into the water. Boil until tender but not mushy, about 6 minutes. Drain and allow to cool somewhat to prevent the asparagus from cooking the eggs upon contact. Cut the spears on the diagonal into 1-inch pieces.

In a bowl, combine the eggs, asparagus, mint, fennel, and salt. Preheat a broiler. In a small, heavy-bottomed, flameproof skillet, warm the olive oil over medium heat. When it is hot enough to make the eggs sizzle, pour in the egg mixture, and use the back of a wooden spoon to even out the mixture in the pan. Reduce the heat to medium low and cook very gently on the bottom, moving the pan around on the burner to ensure even cooking. The heat must not be too high, or the frittata will dry out on the bottom and remain raw in the center. When it is set and cooked on the bottom, after 5 to 7 minutes, remove it from the stove. Slide the pan onto a rack about 9 inches from the broiler element. Leave the oven door ajar and remain with the frittata until it is cooked through and golden on the top, about 4 minutes. Press a finger in the center of the frittata to see if it is firm. If runny, return it to the rack to continue cooking, always watching over it.

Remove the frittata from the broiler and let it cool somewhat, then carefully transfer it to a platter. Allow it to cool to room temperature before serving.

APPETIZERS, SNACKS, AND CONDIMENTS

Tortino with Dandelion Greens or Chicory

tortino con la cicoria

for 4 people as an appetizer
or 2 people for lunch

1 pound young wild dandelion greens,
escarole, or curly endive

4 eggs

2 tablespoons unbleached flour

$^3/_4$ teaspoon sea salt

freshly ground black pepper

6 large cloves garlic, very thinly sliced
lengthwise

6 tablespoons extra-virgin olive oil

An interesting variation on the theme of the frittata is this tortino *made with wild dandelion greens. The main difference between a* frittata *and a* tortino *is that the first contains only eggs and the ingredients that are being bound together with the eggs, usually vegetables, while the* tortino *includes cream in some regions and, in this case, flour. This addition causes the* tortino *to have a somewhat browned, cakelike appearance, echoing the fact that* torta *means "cake." Flour also helps to bind the eggs with the greens, which have a high water content. While the* tortini *I have come across in other parts of Italy are called such also because they are baked, this one is made on the stove top, just like a* frittata. *If you do not have access to wild dandelion greens, chicory or curly endive may be substituted with excellent results.*

Core and wash the greens thoroughly, picking out any yellow or brown leaves and cutting off any roots. Chop coarsely. Allow the water that clings to the leaves to remain; set aside. In a bowl, whisk together the eggs, flour, and salt and season with pepper.

In a skillet with a tight-fitting lid, combine the garlic and 2 tablespoons of the olive oil and warm over medium-low heat until the garlic is softened and lightly colored but not browned, about 6 minutes. Add the greens and toss to coat in the oil. Raise the heat to medium, cover the pan, and cook, stirring occasionally and always returning the cover to the pan, until the greens are wilted and sweet, about 8 minutes. Drain and let cool.

Preheat a broiler. Add the cooled greens to the egg mixture and mix well. In a 10- or 12-inch heavy-bottomed, flameproof skillet or omelet pan, warm the remaining 4 tablespoons olive oil over medium heat. When it is hot

enough to make the eggs sizzle, pour the mixture into the pan, and use the back of a wooden spoon to even out the mixture in the pan. Reduce the heat to medium-low and cook very gently on the bottom, moving the pan around on the surface of the burner to ensure even cooking. It is important that the heat not be too high, or the *tortino* will dry out on the bottom and remain raw in the center. When it is set and cooked on the bottom, after 5 to 7 minutes, remove it from the stove top. Slide the pan onto a rack about 9 inches from the broiler element. Leave the oven door ajar and remain with the *tortino*, watching over it until it is cooked through and golden on the surface, about 5 to 7 minutes, depending upon the width of the pan. To test for doneness, press a finger in the center of the *tortino* to see if it is firm. If it is runny, slide it back onto the rack to continue cooking, always watching over it.

Remove the *tortino* from the broiler and let it cool somewhat, then carefully transfer it to a platter. Allow it to cool to room temperature before serving.

Glutton's Sauce

salsa ghiotta

APPETIZERS, SNACKS, AND CONDIMENTS

makes about 1¾ cups for marinating
or as a table sauce for 2 to 3 pounds meat

1½ cups dry red wine

1½ cups dry white wine

¼ cup red or white wine vinegar

5 tablespoons extra-virgin olive oil

2 ounces prosciutto, minced

¼ small lemon, thinly sliced and peel, pith, and seeds removed

3 fresh sage leaves, or 1 teaspoon dried sage

1 fresh rosemary sprig, or 1 teaspoon crumbled dried rosemary

4 large cloves garlic, crushed but left whole

3 juniper berries, crushed

2 very fresh plump chicken livers, trimmed of any dark spots, fat, and membranes, then chopped, if serving as a table sauce

sea salt

freshly ground black pepper

⤜ *An essential component of the Umbrian table is meat and game grilled over an open fire. The meat is always basted while it cooks to keep it moist and succulent. Salsa ghiotta is used as a basting liquid for lamb, pork, beef, poultry, or game, and as a sauce at the table. There are many variations of this preparation. In those intended for anointing small game birds, the entrails and heads of the birds are simmered slowly in the sauce for as long as two hours, adding a great deal of flavor. Other versions call for stale bread to thicken the sauce. Olives, anchovies, and capers are sometimes included.*

In Umbria, salsa ghiotta is often used first as a marinade and then poured into a leccarda, a traditional rectangular copper vessel fashioned with four low feet. The leccarda is positioned below the roasting meat in order to capture drippings from the roast and to serve as a handy receptacle for continual basting. For use as a table sauce, the sauce is simmered for several minutes after the basting is finished, and then served at the table.

Select an ample nonaluminum saucepan and combine all of the ingredients in the pan except for the livers, salt, and pepper. Place over high heat, bring to a simmer, and cook until reduced by half, about 20 minutes. Pass the mixture through a fine-mesh sieve and return it to the saucepan.

If using the sauce as a marinade or a basting mixture for meat, set the livers aside. Place the meat in a nonaluminum vessel and pour the sauce over the top. Permit the flavors to permeate the flesh, turning the meat every hour or so, until time for cooking. Make extra sauce for basting the meat as it cooks and for serving with the meat at the table.

For using the sauce at the table, reheat it and add the livers. Simmer gently for 5 minutes to cook the livers, and then serve hot. Whether using the sauce for marinating, basting, or as a table sauce, season it to taste with salt and pepper after the meat is cooked, not before.

First Courses of Soups and Pasta

primi

3

It used to be a custom in Terni to throw the cooking water from the ciriole *(long, thick, fresh pasta) on the trunks of trees whose undergrowth sheltered* pioppi, *the wood mushrooms that were used for the sauce, in the belief that the mushrooms would grow in the same spot again.*

—BY WAY OF CARLO GRASSETTI
AND ANNALISA BRESCHI,
La cucina umbra

Despite the sometimes vast differences in regional cooking styles, the custom of eating soup, pasta, or risotto as a first course, or *primo*, is a ritual in Umbria, just as it is everywhere in Italy.

Umbrian soups are typically robust and full of flavor. Soup, pasta, and beans are often put together here, as they are all over the peninsula, but with Umbria's particular flavors. Beans of all kinds—favas, dried peas, chickpeas, chickling peas—are also cooked alone and puréed into luscious soups laced with the wonderful Umbrian olive oil. The same tasty oil is drizzled over steaming bowls of other soups at the table. The heat from the soup releases the clear, wonderful aroma and taste of the raw oil.

The *battuto*—chopped carrot, celery, onion or garlic, various aromatic herbs, and perhaps chopped pancetta, prosciutto, or, less frequently today, lard—is almost always at the base of soups for flavor and substance. Meatless soups need the *battuto* for a boost, while other soups often rely on the tasty pancetta, prosciutto, or lard to act as the meat component.

In Umbria, pasta, too, is hearty. Unlike the delicate *sfoglia*, the handmade egg pasta of Emilia-Romagna in the north, traditional Umbrian pasta, which is still very popular today, consists of nothing more than flour and water. In the past, white flour was unaffordable to most of the population, thus most cooks used whole-wheat and *farro* flours. It is considered heretical to include eggs in the dough, except, perhaps, a single white to help hold together the flour and water. Skilled women pride themselves on being able to make perfectly uniform and workable dough without the crutch of egg whites, using only their hands and the rhythmic movement of their entire bodies. According to an old adage from Spoleto, the dough has to be prepared a *culu mossu*, with continual movement of the rump.

Homemade egg pasta, tagliatelle in particular, was once a food for the privileged, but today it is widespread. Delicate Umbrian sauces, such as those with white truffles, are better-suited to tagliatelle than to the rustic eggless pasta; thus the more refined egg noodle also has its place in the regional cuisine.

Most traditional Umbrian sauces are simple, even elemental, as in *ciriole alla ternana* (page 77), comprised of nothing more than olive oil, tomatoes, and garlic. They are usually vegetable based, and they often rely on foods foraged from the woods and the countryside, like wild asparagus and fennel and many types of field and forest mushrooms.

Only two pastas are indigenous to Umbria. The first, *strangozzi*, also called *stringozze, strengozzi, picchiarelli,* and *tagliatelle,* are long, narrow, flat strands of egg-based pasta. The name *strangozzi* was possibly derived from *stringhe da scarpe,* "shoelaces," which the pasta resembles in length, width, and thickness. To confuse matters further, *strangozzi* are sometimes round rather than flat, making them identical to *umbricelli.*

The second, *umbricelli,* a term used in Perugia, Todi, Orvieto, and a few other scattered areas, are long, thick, round handmade fresh noodles comprised of only flour and water. They are also called *biche, bisciolone* (archaic Perugian dialect), *bigoli* (in Gubbio), *ciriole* or *ceriole* (after the word for small eels, which the thick and slippery pasta texture resembles), *lombrici, spaghettoni, ombricelli,* and *strozzapreti.* (The name of the latter, which means "priest stranglers," reflects the popular irreverence toward the clergy who, other than the rich, were the only people who ate well in the past.) There is sometimes a hole in the middle of *umbricelli,* which causes the sauce to interact with the pasta differently than with pasta that is not hollow, such as spaghetti. The hole causes the eater to take in more air and also allows the sauce to linger longer in the mouth because more skill is employed to master eating without slurping. The experience can be duplicated successfully with factory-made *bucatini.*

Pasta secca, dried pasta, is universal today in Umbria, and it is often used in place of the handmade pastas of the *umbricelli* family. Even black truffles, when they are in season, are paired with *pasta secca.*

Vegetable Soup with Ground Farro

minestra di farro

FIRST COURSES OF SOUPS AND PASTA

for 4 people

5 tablespoons extra-virgin olive oil

2 leeks, including 1 inch of the green tops, all chopped

1 carrot, peeled and minced

1 celery stalk, with leaves, minced

2 tablespoons minced fresh Italian parsley

1 cup ground *farro* (page 16)

2 1/2 quarts ham broth, or other flavorful meat or vegetable broth

sea salt

grated pecorino cheese

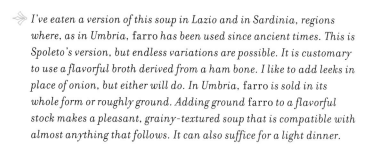

I've eaten a version of this soup in Lazio and in Sardinia, regions where, as in Umbria, farro has been used since ancient times. This is Spoleto's version, but endless variations are possible. It is customary to use a flavorful broth derived from a ham bone. I like to add leeks in place of onion, but either will do. In Umbria, farro is sold in its whole form or roughly ground. Adding ground farro to a flavorful stock makes a pleasant, grainy-textured soup that is compatible with almost anything that follows. It can also suffice for a light dinner.

In a large saucepan or soup pot, warm the olive oil over medium heat. Stir in the vegetables and parsley and sauté slowly until softened, about 10 minutes. Now stir in the *farro* and then pour in the broth. Simmer uncovered, until the *farro* is tender, about 30 minutes.

Check for salt, then ladle into warmed soup plates to serve. Pass the cheese at the table.

Farro is a grain from the mountains. Colfiorito is the best zone for *farro* and chickling peas. The earth is better there for these things.

—FAUSTO TODINI, OWNER, CHEF,
RISTORANTE UMBRIA, TODI

Purée of Fava Beans with Scallions

passato di fave con lo scalogno

for 6 people

¹/₂ pound (1 generous cup) dried fava beans

3 large cloves garlic, halved

¹/₂ teaspoon fennel seeds

sea salt

3 scallions, including 1 inch of the green tops, sliced paper-thin

fruity extra-virgin olive oil for serving

freshly ground coarse black pepper

Fava beans have long been a staple of the poor throughout Italy. In the past, a porridge made from the rehydrated dried beans was standard fare for the contadino, *more often than not consumed as a bracing breakfast before setting out to labor in the fields. Nowadays, a puréed soup of this sort is typically a first course, not the centerpiece of a meal. As the beans alone are relatively mild in flavor, it is essential to use a fruity extra-virgin olive oil, drizzling a little pool of it over the purée, and then sprinkling the lot with paper-thin sweet onion, a veil of sea salt, and plenty of coarsely ground black pepper.*

Pick over the beans, then place in a bowl with water to cover generously. Soak for 24 hours in a cool place, changing the water once or twice.

Drain the beans and place in a saucepan. Add the garlic, fennel seeds, and water to cover by 2 inches. Bring to a boil over high heat, reduce the heat to medium, and simmer gently, uncovered, until the beans are completely softened. The cooking time will depend upon the process by which the beans were dried, how long they were soaked, and the age of the beans. Plan on from forty minutes to 1¹/₂ hours, and add water as necessary to ensure that the beans do not dry out. The object is for the beans to finish cooking in just enough water to form a creamy purée when passed through a food mill; it is best not to end up with so much water that the excess needs to be poured out.

When the beans have cooled somewhat, pass them through a food mill. Alternatively, purée them in a food processor. Add salt to taste. Reheat the purée and pour into individual serving bowls. Top each serving with scallions, plenty of olive oil, and pepper and serve immediately.

Note: A slice of toasted bread rubbed with garlic and anointed with extra-virgin olive oil is often placed at the bottom of each bowl and the soup is ladled over the top.

FIRST COURSES OF SOUPS AND PASTA

Lentil and Rice Soup

minestra di riso e lenticchie

for 6 people

1/2 pound (1 generous cup) brown lentils, preferably Castelluccio type

2 1/2 quarts water or meat broth

1 large bay leaf

1/4 cup fruity extra-virgin olive oil, plus oil for serving (optional)

3 or 4 large cloves garlic, minced

1/4 pound prosciutto, chopped

1 tablespoon minced fresh sage, or 1 teaspoon crumbled dried sage

1 cup peeled, seeded, and chopped canned tomatoes, plus 1 cup of their liquid

1 tablespoon tomato paste

2 teaspoons sea salt

1/2 cup white rice

freshly ground black pepper

3 tablespoons chopped fresh Italian parsley

Lentil soups are typical of the cucina povera—peasant-influenced kitchen—found throughout Italy, but in Umbria lentils are most often paired with rice rather than macaroni in soups. Because there are relatively few ingredients here, and the flavors of lentils and rice are bland on their own, a large amount of garlic is essential, along with a robust, full-bodied extra-virgin olive oil. A meatless version is traditional for lunch or supper on Christian fast days. If using tasty Umbrian lentils and an aromatic olive oil, a meatless version could stand on its own without the flavor boost of the prosciutto.

Pick over the lentils and rinse well. Place them in a saucepan or soup pot and add the water or broth and the bay leaf. Bring to a boil over medium heat, immediately reduce the heat to medium-low, and simmer gently, uncovered, until they are half-cooked, about 12 minutes.

Meanwhile, in a cold skillet, combine the olive oil and garlic and place over medium-low heat. Sauté until the oil begins to heat and the garlic softens somewhat, about 4 minutes. Stir in the prosciutto and sauté gently for another minute or two until the garlic is fully softened. Now add the sage, the tomatoes and their liquid, and the tomato paste. Simmer for 5 minutes to blend the flavors, then transfer the tomato mixture to the pan with the lentils. Bring to a boil and add the salt and the rice. Stir well and cook over medium heat, uncovered, until the rice and lentils are tender, about 15 minutes.

Season with the pepper and stir in the parsley. Ladle into warmed soup plates. Add a drizzle of olive oil to each serving at the table, if desired.

Pumpkin Soup with Escarole and Farro

minestra di zucca con scarola e farro

for 4 people

5 tablespoons extra-virgin olive oil, plus oil for serving (optional)

2 large cloves garlic, sliced or bruised

1 onion, chopped

1 leafy fresh sage sprig, about 9 inches long, or equivalent smaller sage sprigs, or 1 teaspoon crumbled dried sage leaves

1 cup *farro* (page 16)

3/4-pound piece eating pumpkin, butternut squash, or calabaza, peeled, seeded, and diced (about 1/2 pound diced)

2 1/2 quarts meat or vegetable broth

6 ounces escarole (heart and leaves), roughly chopped

sea salt

freshly ground black pepper

This is an adaptation of a recipe from Clarisse Schiller, founder of Cucina Viva gastronomical retreat and cooking school in Campello sul Clitunno. Umbrian zucca, or "pumpkin," is similar to American butternut squash or to calabaza, the West Indian pumpkin ubiquitous in Latin and Caribbean markets. The natural sweetness of the pumpkin or squash unites happily with the escarole, which, although bitter in its uncooked state, becomes quite sweet with cooking. The combination is smashing. The nutty, tender farro kernels are what make the soup particularly Umbrian. I advise using homemade meat or vegetable broth rather than water for greater flavor. It is preferable to use a fresh sprig of sage, which is taken out after the soup cooks, but dried crumbled sage may be substituted.

In a soup pot, warm together the oil and garlic over medium-low heat until the garlic is fragrant and wilted but not colored, about 2 minutes. Add the onion and fresh or dried sage and sauté gently, stirring frequently, until the onion is softened but not deeply colored, 8 to 10 minutes. Stir in the *farro* and sauté for about 1 minute to coat with the oil. Add the pumpkin or squash and continue to sauté until it begins to sweat, about 10 minutes.

Pour in the broth, stirring to mix, and bring to a boil. Reduce the heat to medium-low and simmer uncovered, stirring occasionally, until the pumpkin or squash and the *farro* are cooked, about 45 minutes. The hulls of the *farro* grains ensures their chewiness, even after cooking, but the center should be tender. If fresh sage has been used, remove and discard. Stir in the escarole and simmer until it is tender but not falling apart, about 5 minutes longer.

Season with salt and pepper. Ladle into warmed soup plates. Add a drizzle of olive oil to each serving, if desired.

Etruscan Soup

zuppa etrusca

for 4 people

2$^1/_2$ cups (scant 1 pound) chickling peas (page 15)

baking soda

1$^1/_4$ cups ($^1/_2$ pound) *farro* (page 16)

5 tablespoons high-quality extra-virgin olive oil, plus oil for serving

4 large cloves garlic, minced

6 ounces prosciutto, chopped

6 fresh rosemary sprigs, tied together, or 2 teaspoons crumbled dried rosemary

1 tablespoon chopped fresh marjoram, or 1 teaspoon crumbled dried marjoram

1$^1/_2$ teaspoons sea salt, or to taste

freshly ground black pepper

Fausto Todini's restaurant, Ristorante Umbria, dates back to 1300. He has operated it for forty-five years, and his father ran it before him. Customers can eat in the rustic, frescoed dining room, or, in warm weather, alfresco on the balcony overlooking Todi's beautiful panorama.

Rinse the chickling peas, then place in a bowl with plenty of water to cover. Add a pinch of baking soda and let soak for 2 days, changing the water several times during that time and adding a pinch of baking soda to each new batch.

Rinse the *farro*, then place in a bowl with plenty of water to cover and let soak overnight.

Drain the chickling peas and place in a saucepan with water to cover by 4 to 5 inches. Bring to a boil, reduce the heat to medium, and simmer gently, uncovered, until very tender, about 50 minutes. Remove from the heat and let cool somewhat, then drain, reserving the liquid.

Purée the peas, adding some of the cooking liquid to produce a thin purée. It is best to use a food mill fitted with the attachment with large holes for puréeing, as the thin skins of the peas will be left behind. Lacking a food mill, use a food processor, but be sure to purée thoroughly. Reserve for use later.

In a cold skillet, combine the olive oil and the garlic and place over medium-low heat. Sauté until the oil begins to heat and the garlic softens somewhat, about 4 minutes. Stir in the prosciutto, rosemary, and marjoram and sauté gently just until the garlic is fully softened, a few minutes

longer. If using fresh rosemary, remove and discard
the sprigs.

Combine the pea purée and the *soffritto* of garlic,
prosciutto and herbs, and pass them together through the
food mill. It will be necessary to add several ladles of
the cooking liquid when passing the mixture through the
mill. Return the purée to a saucepan with some of its
cooking liquid and stir in the *farro*. Bring to a boil over
medium heat, then reduce the heat to medium-low and
simmer very gently until the *farro* is tender and the soup
has thickened to a hearty but not stodgy texture, about
30 minutes, adding more of the cooking liquid as necessary
to prevent the soup from drying out. Stir in the salt.

Ladle the soup into warmed soup plates. Pass a veil of the
pepper over each serving, then drizzle a little pool of
extra-virgin olive oil atop each serving. The soup should
be eaten steaming hot.

Handmade Umbricelli

umbricelli

makes 1 pound; for 4 people

3 cups unbleached flour, plus flour for working the dough

about 1 cup water

6 quarts water and 3 tablespoons coarse sea salt for cooking

This is Umbria's thick fresh pasta made without eggs, described on page 64. It should only be cooked fresh, although it is commonly seen in a packaged dried form in boutique food shops all over the region. Umbricelli in that form are only a novelty, however. Once they are dry, they never cook up to tenderness again, instead remaining hard in the center, no matter how long they boil. Umbricelli are easy to make at home. The sauces of tradition for marrying with this pasta include a succulent goose ragù loved by the Umbrians, a rich tomato-sausage blend, and a simple sauce of truffles.

FACING PAGE:
Maestra pastaia making umbricelli at the Frantoio Menconi, Campello sul Clitunno on tour with Cucina Viva (page 156)

If making the pasta by hand, form the flour in a mound on a large work surface. Use your hand to make a well in the center. Pour 1 cup water into the well without permitting it to run out. Using a fork, gradually draw all the flour into the water in the well until a workable dough is formed. If necessary, sprinkle the dough with more water to make it pliable. It will be somewhat tough, but this is the rustic nature of the pasta. Shape into a ball.

If using a food processor, combine the flour and 1 cup water in the processor and engage the motor until a dough forms. If necessary, add a little more water to form a workable dough. Shape into a ball.

Prepare the work surface so that it is free of any bits of dough. Sprinkle it with flour. Flatten the ball of dough into a disk ½ inch thick. With a large chef's knife, cut the disk into strips about 1 inch wide. Then cut the strips into 1-inch cubes. Working with 1 cube at a time, roll it gently between your palms to form a long, thick cord about the length of a rod of spaghetti and about ⅛ inch thick. As the strands are formed, set them aside on kitchen towels and cover with more kitchen towels. Allow the pasta to rest for about 45 minutes, but no longer than several hours.

To cook the pasta, bring the 6 quarts water to a rolling boil in a large pot. Pick up the four corners of the towels with the *umbricelli* still in them and slide them directly into the boiling water. Add the salt to the water immediately. Allow the water to come back to a boil over the highest heat possible. As soon as it boils, the pasta should be done. Drain, combine with the sauce, and serve hot.

Penci with Sausage, Lemon, and Nutmeg Sauce

penci di Cascia

for 2 to 4 people

1 egg

$^1/_8$ teaspoon freshly ground black pepper, or to taste

pinch of freshly grated nutmeg

juice of $^1/_2$ lemon

grated zest of 1 small lemon

$^1/_4$ cup heavy cream

4 tablespoons extra-virgin olive oil

2 ounces lean pancetta, diced

2 lean sweet Italian pork sausages, casings removed and crumbled

4 quarts water

$^1/_2$ pound Handmade *Umbricelli* (page 75) or *bucatini*

2 tablespoons coarse sea salt

grated pecorino cheese for serving

According to one source, this hearty recipe is from the mountainous city of Cascia, while Umbrian food writer and culinary historian Rita Boini places its origin in the Spoleto carnival celebration, circa 1494. The sauce is used with handmade penci, another name for umbricelli. Follow the recipe carefully in order to prevent the sauce from overcooking.

In a bowl, lightly beat together the egg, pepper, nutmeg, lemon juice, lemon zest, and cream. Set aside.

In a large, deep, heavy-bottomed skillet, warm 1 tablespoon of the oil over medium heat. Add the pancetta and sauté until it colors, 4 to 5 minutes. Remove from the heat and transfer the pancetta to a bowl; set aside.

Return the skillet to medium heat and reheat the oil. Add the sausage and sauté until colored, about 6 minutes. Remove the pan from the heat and transfer the sausage to the bowl with the pancetta. Drain off all excess fat and add the remaining 3 tablespoons olive oil to the skillet. Set the skillet aside.

Bring the water to a rapid boil in a large pot. Add the pasta and the salt and stir well. If you are using fresh pasta, when the water returns to a boil, drain the pasta. If you are using *bucatini*, follow package instructions to cook them al dente, usually about 8 minutes, then drain the pasta. In either case, reserve about 1 cup of the cooking water.

Just before the pasta is ready, return the skillet to medium heat and warm the oil. Have ready a warmed large, shallow bowl. Return the pancetta and sausage to the skillet. At the moment the pasta is drained, add it to the skillet and toss it with the sausage and pancetta. Remove from the heat and add the egg mixture. Stir quickly until the egg coats the pasta; the egg will continue to cook from the heat of the pasta. Transfer the contents of the skillet to the warmed bowl, adding some of the reserved water to the pasta to thin out the sauce if necessary. Serve the pasta piping hot. Pass the pecorino at the table.

Ciriole with Quick Tomato Sauce

ciriole alla ternana con la salsa di pomodoro

for 4 people

FOR THE SAUCE:

$2^1/_2$ cups peeled, seeded, and chopped fresh or canned plum tomatoes

2 large cloves garlic, minced

5 tablespoons extra-virgin olive oil

$^1/_2$ teaspoon sea salt

freshly ground white or black pepper

6 quarts water

1 pound Handmade *Umbricelli* (page 75) or *bucatini*

2 tablespoons coarse sea salt

If a *sagra* is really a "ceremonial festival originally celebrating the anniversary of a church or a cathedral," and in addition to its religious overtones also has the responsibility of sustaining an ancient tradition (culinary—much more important than religious!), then it seems to me the *umbricelli* shouldn't be squeezed out of a machine, but rather rolled and cut again and cut again.

— Thomas Briccetti, Perugia, 1977

Ciriole, *the handmade pasta of Terni, are the same as the handmade pastas of other Umbrian provinces. In Terni, the sauce may be a simple one based on tomatoes, or one of* funghi di pioppo *(wood mushrooms), tomatoes, basil, and, if available, mussels! I offer the first, almost with hesitation due to its simplicity, but as most Americans resort to bottled tomato sauces, a sauce as simple and as good as this one should circulate to give courage to the faint-hearted. As with all dishes where very few ingredients are used, it is essential that each be of the highest quality, as there are no other supporting flavors. That means high-quality, thick-walled, and meaty plum tomatoes, whether fresh or canned, fresh garlic, and excellent fruity extra-virgin olive oil. Grated cheese does not usually accompany this dish.* Bucatini *may be substituted for handmade* ciriole, *which is simply another name for Umbria's classic* umbricelli.

To make the sauce, in a heavy-bottomed saucepan, combine the tomatoes, garlic, and 2 tablespoons of the olive oil. Bring to a boil over high heat and continue to cook a *fuoco vivace,* that is, over a lively flame, until thickened, about 20 minutes.

Meanwhile, bring the water to a rapid boil in a large pot. Just before the sauce is ready, add the pasta and the salt to the boiling water and stir well. If you are using fresh pasta, when the water returns to a boil, drain the pasta; it should be cooked through. If you are using *bucatini,* follow the package directions to cook them al dente, usually about 8 minutes (because they are hollow, *bucatini* overcook in an instant, so watch the pot carefully). Drain and pour into a warmed large, shallow bowl.

Stir the salt, pepper to taste, and the remaining 3 tablespoons olive oil into the sauce, then pour the sauce over the pasta. Toss well and serve at once.

Clarisse Schiller's Pasta with Asparagus Sauce

*pasta con sugo di asparagi
alla Clarisse Schiller*

for 4 people

1 pound asparagus, preferably pencil-thin

5 quarts water

2 tablespoons coarse salt

6 tablespoons extra-virgin olive oil,
plus several tablespoons to finish

1 large bunch wild scallions, or 4 bunches
cultivated scallions, including 3 inches of the
green tops, thinly sliced on the diagonal

generous pinch of red pepper flakes

1 pound *pennette* or other small pasta
(see recipe introduction)

My friend Clarisse Schiller, who lives in the tiny
medieval village of Lizori above Campello sul
Clitunno, makes this pasta when the wild asparagus that grow on her land are in season, but I have
made it successfully with cultivated asparagus
by increasing the quantity of fresh herbs. Of course,
there is no comparison between the taste of wild
and cultivated asparagus, but with spears harvested at the height of the season, high-quality olive
oil, and more scallions than would otherwise be
necessary, a good replica of the original recipe
is possible. Clarisse uses cipollaccio, wild scallions, which I find easily enough in my area in
April and May, but cultivated scallions will also do.
It is very important to use the best quality extra-
virgin olive oil you can afford. The ideal pasta
cuts for the sauce are orecchiette, pennette (short
penne), gemelli (twins), or a similar tubular
short macaroni cut.

Trim off the tough ends of the asparagus. If the spears are
not perfectly fresh and tender, beginning near the base
of each spear, peel away the thicker skin to reveal the
tender stalk underneath, stopping within a few inches of
the tip. Cut on the diagonal into 2-inch pieces.

Bring the water to a rapid boil in a large pot. Add the salt
and the asparagus at once and boil for 5 minutes.
Meanwhile, in a skillet large enough to accommodate the
pasta later, warm the 6 tablespoons oil over medium
heat and stir in the scallions and red pepper flakes. Using
a wire skimmer or sieve, scoop out all the asparagus pieces
and add them to the skillet with the scallions. Do not
discard the water. Toss the ingredients together and sauté
until the asparagus pieces are sweet and tender, 1 to
2 minutes. They must not be crunchy. Remove the skillet
from the heat.

Return the water to a rapid boil and stir in the pasta.
Cook until al dente. The timing will depend upon the type
of pasta used. Drain the pasta and add it to the hot skillet
with the asparagus and scallions. Toss well and check for
salt. Pour in several tablespoons of olive oil, toss again,
and transfer to a warmed large, shallow bowl. Serve
immediately.

Note: No grated cheese tops the pasta at the table if the
asparagus are fresh and tasty. It is better to add more
flavor with good raw olive oil and even a pinch more red
pepper flakes at the end than to detract from the asparagus by introducing cheese.

The Mill that Grinds Wheat the Ancient Way

Cease your grinding,
you women who work at the mill,
sleep late,
even though cockcrow is heralding the dawn.
For Demetrius has commanded the nymphs
to do the work of your hands, and they, by jumping down
make it turn upon its axis,
that, with its rotating spokes,
it may move the heavy concave millstones.

—ANTIPATER OF MACEDONIA, EARLY FIRST CENTURY B.C.

In Umbria, a revival of the ancient methods for milling grains
has been taking place. After the durum wheat is grown and
harvested, it is brought to a mill that specializes in grinding in
the age-old way. The Mulino Silvestri in Torgiano, a medieval
town built on a rise where the Tiber and Chiascio Rivers meet
south of Perugia, is such a mill. It is run by Vinicio Silvestri and
his three sons, Tigellino, Sergio, and Ivano, and I went to visit
it with my friend Paolo Destefanis.

The mill's massive stone tower loomed on the banks of the Tiber
as we approached, and Paolo spoke admiringly of the masonry
skills that have allowed the building to endure for over nine
hundred years. The original main structure is where the water
turbine, once a wheel, exploits the seven-foot drop in the
riverbed, thus producing the energy to move the millstones.

For many years, Paolo has been coming here with his neighbor
Ulisse, an organic-wheat farmer in nearby Tuscany, and he
knows the men well. Vinicio tells Paolo that the *mulino* has been
the Silvestri family business for over three centuries, long
enough to have supplied the flour for many popes, by which he
means the pontifical armies who defended the northern border
of their dominion.

Thomas Briccetti's Spaghetti in the Style of Norcia

spaghetti alla norcina di Thomas Briccetti

for 4 to 6 people

2 ounces dried porcino mushrooms

1 cup hot water

5 tablespoons extra-virgin olive oil

2 onions, minced

1 pound lean sweet Italian pork sausage meat

1 teaspoon ground fennel

pinch of red pepper flakes

pinch of freshly grated nutmeg

$1/2$ cup heavy cream

fine sea salt

6 quarts water

1 pound spaghetti or *lumache* (medium shell pasta)

2 tablespoons coarse sea salt

My friend, Thomas Briccetti, was a maestro, *and indeed everyone called him that. He had conducted symphonies in America for twenty-five years before he moved to Perugia, where he began to compose music. Ours is an adventurous tale full of fun, good food, and wine. When he died, he left behind many admirers, much music, and an opera. He always said that cooking was as full of art as music was, but he left behind only one recorded gastronomical piece,* spaghetti alla norcina.

Place the mushrooms in a bowl with the hot water and let stand until softened, about 30 minutes. Drain the mushrooms, reserving the soaking liquid. Strain the liquid through a fine-mesh sieve lined with cheesecloth or a paper towel, and set aside. Chop the mushrooms.

In an ample skillet, warm 2 tablespoons of the oil over medium-low heat. Add the onions and mushrooms and sauté until the onions are well softened but not browned, about 7 minutes. Meanwhile, in a smaller skillet, warm the remaining 3 tablespoons olive oil over medium-low heat and add the crumbled sausage. Sauté, using a wooden spoon to break up the sausage as it browns, until it is nicely colored but not hardened, about 8 minutes. Stir in the fennel. Add the sausage to the onion mixture along with the red pepper flakes and stir well. Raise the heat to medium and add the reserved mushroom liquid. Simmer to permit excess water to evaporate, about 5 minutes. Stir in the nutmeg and cream and cook until thickened, about 3 minutes. Taste and adjust with fine sea salt.

Meanwhile, bring the water to a rapid boil in a large pot. Add the pasta and the coarse salt, stir well, and boil until al dente. The timing will depend upon the type of pasta used. Drain the pasta and transfer to a warmed large, shallow bowl. Pour on the sauce, toss well, and serve immediately.

Second Courses with Meat

secondi di carne

4

In the past, the prevalent poverty of most of Italy and the arid geography of the southern regions discouraged a meat culture. As a result, Italy is not generally known for its meat. But in Umbria, Italy's "great green heart," there are lush pastures for cattle, sheep, goats, and pigs, and its thick forests teem with all kinds of game. The region is also known for the quality of its farm-raised meat.

Travelers to Italy are confused by the many terms used for beef on menus. It was from Paolo Buitoni, patriarch of Umbria's oldest food-producing family and now a cattle rancher, that I finally learned what distinguishes *vitello*, *vitellone*, *manzo*, *bue*, and *bistecca*. *Bue*, though rarely encountered today, is from a three- to five-year-old draft animal that has been castrated. *Vitello* is always a milk-fed calf no older than six months. Once the calf is fed grain, its meat is no longer pink-beige and is instead red. *Vitellone* is synonymous with *manzo*, "beef," which in Italy denotes meat from cattle that are slaughtered between eighteen and nineteen months. Finally, a *bistecca* is a beef steak. The famous *bistecca fiorentina* from the Chianina cattle that were once part of the Tuscan and west Umbrian landscape is no longer derived from the huge Chianina cattle, which yielded little meat in relation to their overall weight. Today, *bistecca fiorentina* invariably comes from cattle breeds other than the Chianina.

Pork in Umbria is first-rate, and is considered by many to be the best in Italy. Many farmers still raise and butcher their own pigs, and local winter festivals throughout Umbria continue to mark the importance of the pig in Umbrian culture.

But *porchetta* (roasted suckling pig) reigns supreme over all the delicious Umbrian pork dishes. It is an ancient culinary tradition that is inevitably practiced in public—at festivals, for celebrations, at carnival time, and such—and it is a ubiquitous spectacle on the streets from central to southern Italy, where it is peddled in pushcarts or sold on the roadside from trucks. Umbria's version is most often stuffed with wild fennel, rosemary, garlic, and black pepper, the aromas of which penetrate the meat as it cooks slowly on a revolving spit.

Most meats are roasted *allo spiedo*, "on the spit." But the predominance of game has naturally brought about a grassroots expertise in succulent cooking methods, including stewing, pan roasting, and braising.

Still other techniques are used in meat cookery to make tough cuts tasty, including cocooning them in thin layers of lard or in prosciutto, in preparation for the spit or the roasting pan, and cutting them into small pieces for sautéing with a mixture of chopped pancetta and wild fennel or marjoram.

Related to pork but not much like it in flavor is wild boar. Like the wild deer in America, boar ravage gardens and are the scourge of farmers. Boar hunting is only permitted two months of the year by Italian law. The meat is prized for eating. Boar is baked and roasted, and appears in stews, sausages, sauces, and ragù.

Hare, duck, pheasant, quail, pigeon, thrush, and many other wild bird varieties that make good eating are commonplace as well. The more tender of these are roasted *allo spiedo* over a wood-burning fire, in the quintessential Umbrian manner, and kept moist with aromatic olive oil-based basting sauces.

Rabbit is popular, too, and is as good when cooked properly as it is bad when overcooked. When not well larded and spit-roasted, it is fried like chicken, steam-roasted in a pot on the stove top, made into endless variations of stew, cooked gently until it falls off the bone into a sauce for pasta, or incorporated into a *salmì* (marinated, then stewed).

Finally, there is a marked taste for goose, a phenomenon that probably goes back to the Etruscans. In ancient Etruria, the goose was valued not only as a food, but also as a symbol of domestic tranquility. In the most popular preparation, the bird is cooked slowly for a long time in a sauce with tomato and olive oil and local herbs until the meat virtually falls off the bones, which produces a *ragù* usually reserved for thick, handmade pasta (page 75).

A recent trend is the importance of turkey. I have found the flavor of turkey in Umbria to be quite different and more delicate than elsewhere. It is typically cooked on the stove top rather than roasted.

Squab in the Umbrian Style

piccioni all'umbra

for 4 people

4 squabs with their giblets

5 tablespoons extra-virgin olive oil

3 large cloves garlic, bruised

6 fresh sage sprigs, 3 inches long

6 fresh rosemary sprigs, 3 inches long

6 whole cloves

zest of $1/2$ lemon, in large strips

1 cup dry white wine

5 to 6 tablespoons white wine vinegar

$1/2$ teaspoon sea salt, or to taste

freshly ground black pepper

4 slices coarse country bread

➤ Piccioni, *farm-raised young pigeons, or squabs, between three and four weeks old, are tender and tasty. Cooking them this way is typical throughout Umbria, with variations that include anchovy tucked into the cavity or larding with pancetta. Butchers often deprive customers of the giblets of fowl, but for this dish, the giblets—heart, gizzard, and liver—are absolutely essential to the sauce. Without them, the sauce is insipid. Serve a slice of coarse country bread or* torta al testo *alongside each bird so as not to waste any of the delicious pan juices. Cornish hens may be substituted.*

Rinse the squabs and dry well inside and out. Trim the giblets of any dark spots, fat, and membrane and chop roughly; set aside. Use kitchen string to tie the legs of each squab loosely together.

In a heavy-bottomed, wide, deep skillet or Dutch oven large enough to accommodate the 4 birds, warm the oil and garlic together over medium-low heat . Sauté until the garlic is nicely golden, about 4 minutes. Tie the sage and rosemary sprigs together with kitchen string and add to the pan along with the cloves, lemon zest, and chopped giblets. Sauté until the giblets are nicely browned, 10 to 12 minutes.

Remove and discard the garlic, raise the heat to medium, and add the birds; brown them evenly, about 15 minutes. Add the wine, vinegar, salt, and pepper to taste and deglaze the pan, stirring to dislodge any bits stuck to the bottom. Cover, reduce the heat to medium-low, and cook until the squabs are tender, about 15 minutes longer, adding a few tablespoons of water, when necessary, to keep the birds moist. Be sure not to overcook them, or their meat will dry out.

Scoop out and discard the bundled herbs, cloves, and lemon zest from the pan juices and check for seasoning. Remove the pan from the heat and let the birds settle for 10 minutes. Meanwhile, toast the bread. Remove the strings from the birds. Serve each squab on a plate alongside a slice of bread. Defat the pan juices and pour over each serving.

Chicken Roasted in the Manner of Suckling Pig

pollo arrosto alla porchetta

for 4 people

1 free-range or organic chicken, about 3 pounds

sea salt

freshly ground black pepper

liver from the chicken, trimmed of any dark spots, fat and membranes, then chopped

$^1/_4$ pound pancetta, chopped

1 tablespoon chopped fresh rosemary, or 1$^1/_2$ teaspoons dried crumbled rosemary

heart and tender leaves of 1 fennel bulb, chopped

2 large cloves garlic, minced

small bunch fresh rosemary (optional)

$^1/_4$ cup extra-virgin olive oil

Cooking chicken on the stove top is a common method throughout Italy. What makes this preparation characteristically Umbrian is the combination of aromatics that is stuffed inside the cavity of the bird to season it. The flavors of wild fennel, rosemary, garlic, and pancetta permeate the meat as it cooks. After the whole chicken has finished cooking and has settled, it is cut into serving pieces and returned to the pan with all of its generous "stuffing," which becomes part of a richly flavored and textured sauce.

Rinse the chicken and dry well inside and out. Sprinkle the inside of the chicken lightly with salt and pepper. In a bowl, combine the liver, pancetta, chopped or dried rosemary, fennel, and garlic and stir to mix. Spoon the mixture into the cavity. Using a kitchen needle and thread, or metal trussing skewers and kitchen string, carefully secure the cavity closed to prevent the stuffing from spilling out during roasting. If using the rosemary bunch, hold the sprigs together parallel to one another and wind kitchen string from one end to the other to prevent the leaves from separating from the sprigs.

Select an ample Dutch oven or heavy-bottomed, wide, deep skillet with a tight-fitting lid. Put the oil and the rosemary bundle, if using, over medium heat. Be certain that the surface of the chicken is dried well to ensure that it will sear and brown nicely. When the oil is hot enough to make the chicken sizzle loudly upon contact, lower the chicken into the pan. Adjust the heat as needed to prevent burning and brown until it is a deep gold all over, turning it when necessary to expose all of the skin to the pan surface. Use two wooden spoons when turning the bird to prevent puncturing it, and losing some of the natural juices. The browning process will take about 20 minutes. Place the lid securely atop the pan and adjust the heat to low. Cook until the chicken is just cooked through and the juices run clear when a thigh joint is pierced, about 45 minutes, turning it occasionally onto each side, but not breast-side down, again with the help of two wooden spoons. I find that if the breast of the bird does not come into direct contact with the pan surface again after the initial browning phase, the breast meat remains moist and juicy.

When the bird is cooked, lift it from the pan, sprinkle with salt to taste, and allow it to settle for 10 to 15 minutes. Remove the string or skewers, cut the chicken into serving pieces, and return the pieces to the pan. Spoon the stuffing from the cavity over the chicken pieces, and check for seasoning. Serve at once directly from the pan.

Roasted Feast-Day Goose
l'oca delle feste arrosto

The popularity of goose in Umbria goes back to the Etruscans. It was a symbol of vigilance, of the faithful guardian, evidenced by the carving of fifty female geese on a sarcophagus unearthed near Norcia. Geese were nourished on "succulent figs," which made their livers particularly tasty. In the cold season, the meat was salted and cured much like pork is today in Umbria. Its rendered fat was preserved for use in cooking.

Overnight, marinate 500 grams [1 pound] of boiled chestnuts, the liver of the goose, four or five chicken livers, and two truffles in a glass of white wine. The day after, warm the wine with its contents until the livers are cooked and chop the chicken livers, truffles, and goose livers. Add two fresh sausages. Fill the cavity of a large goose with this mixture. On a rack, brown the goose over the fire to color it, then roast it for a couple of hours, always on a rack so that the fat drains off. During cooking, use a fork to puncture the goose. Baste it often during cooking with the white wine from the marinade.

—A Norcia area recipe from *Etruscology in guida alla Cucina Etrusca,* by Clotilde Vesco

Fried Chicken Marinated in Sage, Rosemary, and Garlic

pollo fritto all'umbra

for 4 people

1 free-range or organic chicken, about 3 pounds, cut into serving pieces and each breast half cut in half

3 large cloves garlic, finely minced

1 teaspoon finely minced fresh sage, or $^1/_4$ teaspoon crumbled dried sage

$^1/_2$ teaspoon finely minced fresh rosemary, or $^1/_4$ teaspoon crumbled dried rosemary

3 tablespoons extra-virgin olive oil

about $1^1/_2$ cups unbleached flour

3 eggs, or as needed

corn oil for frying

sea salt

→ *There is no equal to the flavor and lightness of traditional Umbrian fried chicken, not even when compared with the best egg-marinated fried rabbit of Tuscany. The meat is seasoned with garlic, sage, rosemary, and fruity olive oil first, which adds a splendid flavor dimension altogether unique to fried chicken. Rabbit can receive the same treatment.*

Rinse the chicken pieces and dry well. In a large bowl, combine the chicken, garlic, sage, rosemary, and olive oil, using your hands to work the herbs into the meat. Cover the bowl tightly with plastic wrap and refrigerate for several hours or up to overnight. Set the chicken out at room temperature for 1 hour before cooking.

Spread out the flour on a sheet of waxed paper or on a platter. Beat the 3 eggs in a wide bowl. Have ready a large, wide platter lined with a double layer of paper towels.

Pour the corn oil to a depth of about 1 inch in a large, heavy-bottomed skillet and warm over medium heat until a crust of bread dropped into it sizzles upon contact. Just before you are ready to begin frying, lightly dredge each piece of chicken in the flour. Dip the chicken piece into the beaten eggs to coat, then dredge it lightly in the flour once again. (If the chicken is coated in flour and egg and left to sit for even a few minutes, the coating will become soggy and the chicken will not fry up crisp and light.)

Slip the chicken pieces into the hot oil, piece by piece. Do not crowd the pan with too many chicken pieces at once, or they will not cook evenly and properly. Fry until golden and thoroughly cooked through to the bone, about 10 minutes in total for each piece, depending on the size. Transfer to the paper towels. Turn each piece of chicken over on the paper in order to ensure that excess oil is absorbed from both sides.

When all of the chicken is cooked and drained, remove the paper towels from the platter, sprinkle the chicken with salt, and serve immediately.

Turkey, Hunter's Style

tacchino alla cacciatora

for 4 people

2 turkey thighs, 1^1/$_2$ pounds each

^{1}/$_4$ cup extra-virgin olive oil

6 large cloves garlic, crushed but left whole

1 fresh rosemary sprig, about 8 inches long,
or 1 teaspoon crumbled dried rosemary

^{3}/$_4$ cup dry white wine

^{1}/$_2$ cup meat broth, or as needed

4 large fresh sage leaves, minced,
or ^{1}/$_2$ teaspoon crumbled dried sage

8 juniper berries, ground

^{3}/$_4$ teaspoon sea salt, or to taste

freshly ground black pepper

Saw or hack each thigh through the bone into 3 pieces. Rinse the turkey pieces and dry well. In a heavy-bottomed, large, wide skillet ample enough to accommodate the turkey pieces without crowding, combine the oil, garlic, and the rosemary, if using sprig. Place over medium-low heat and warm gently, pressing down occasionally with a wooden spoon to release the flavors from the garlic and the rosemary. Do not allow the garlic to color beyond a golden hue. This should take 5 or 6 minutes. Discard the garlic and the rosemary sprigs.

Raise the heat to a fairly lively temperature and slip the turkey pieces into the skillet. Brown them on all sides, about 15 minutes. Add the wine and let the alcohol evaporate, about 3 minutes. Now add the ½ cup broth, the rosemary (if using dried), the sage, and the juniper berries, stirring to distribute all the ingredients. Reduce the heat to low, cover, and cook until the turkey is tender, about 45 minutes. Remove the cover occasionally to stir the meat in order to prevent sticking, re-covering the pan each time. If the turkey seems to be drying out, add more broth as needed to keep it well bathed in cooking liquid.

When the turkey is thoroughly tender, salt and pepper to taste. Transfer to a warmed platter and serve immediately.

Turkey, wild or farm-raised, is eaten throughout Umbria, although not in the English or American manner of stuffing and roasting. For one thing, the bird is not grown to such a large size in Italy, and the female, or hen turkey, is preferred over the male bird because of its tenderness. I feel that this recipe, among the many that exist in the area, is the tastiest way to prepare the bird, particularly for anyone, like me, who favors the dark meat of the turkey. Any of the joints may be used, including the legs or wings, but I prefer the thigh, which is meatier. Have the butcher cut each thigh with a butcher's saw or cleaver.

Donatella's Angry Chicken

pollo all'arrabbiata di Donatella Platoni

for 2 to 4 people

2 young free-range or organic chickens with giblets, $1^1/_2$ to 2 pounds each, cut into serving pieces, or 1 larger free-range or organic chicken with giblets, about 3 pounds, cut into serving pieces

1 small bunch fresh rosemary, or $^1/_2$ teaspoon crumbled dried rosemary

5 tablespoons extra virgin olive oil

6 large cloves garlic, crushed but left whole

1 small dried red chile, or pinch of red pepper flakes

$^1/_2$ small onion, cut into wedges with core attached

$^3/_4$ cup dry white wine

$^3/_4$ cup peeled, seeded, and chopped plum tomatoes

$^1/_2$ teaspoon sea salt, or to taste

Donatella Platoni invited me to her country house near Perugia to eat this peppery chicken stew. When I arrived, she was talking to the butcher on the telephone and holding the chickens he had just delivered. The stomachs of these birds showed no trace of grain, the proof that they have been properly fed. She reprimanded the butcher for this, and for cutting them up with a knife instead of a cleaver. Small, cleavered pieces are more manageable with a fork and knife. Donatella sent back the birds and a new batch came back within the hour.

Rinse the chicken pieces and dry well. Trim any dark spots, fat, and membrane from the liver(s) and heart(s) and cut them into quarters. Trim the tough outer layer from the gizzard(s) and chop. If using the rosemary bunch, hold the sprigs together parallel to one another and wind kitchen string from one end to the other to prevent the leaves from separating from the sprigs. Set the chicken, giblets, and rosemary bundle aside.

In a cold, deep, heavy-bottomed skillet large enough to accommodate the chicken without crowding (or use two smaller skillets), combine the olive oil, garlic, and whole chile or red pepper flakes and warm over medium-low heat. When the oil is hot enough to make the onion sizzle, add the onion and rosemary bundle or dried rosemary and sauté gently until the mixture is aromatic and the garlic and onion are nicely softened but not browned, about 8 minutes. At this point, add the chicken and giblets, raise the heat to medium, and sauté to brown nicely on all sides, about 20 minutes.

Pour in the wine and use a wooden spoon to stir all the ingredients together, taking care not to puncture the chicken pieces or break them up. Use gentle motions to detach any piece that may stick to the bottom of the pan, so as to leave all the pieces intact. When the alcohol has evaporated, after about 3 minutes, add the tomatoes, distributing them evenly. Reduce the heat to medium-low and cook until the chicken is tender, about 20 minutes longer.

Season with the salt and transfer to a warmed platter. Serve the chicken very hot.

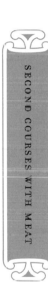

SECOND COURSES WITH MEAT

Chicken, Hunter's Style Ristorante Cibocchi

pollo al Ristorante Cibocchi

for 2 to 3 people

1 free-range or organic chicken with giblets, about 3$^1/_2$ pounds, cut into serving pieces

6 tablespoons extra-virgin olive oil

5 cloves garlic, minced

2 teaspoons minced fresh rosemary, or 1 teaspoon crumbled dried rosemary

1 teaspoon minced fresh sage, or $^1/_2$ teaspoon crumbled dried sage

$^1/_2$ onion, chopped

$^1/_4$ pound (about 1 cup) Umbrian, Ligurian, or other high-quality tart green olives, pitted and sliced

1 cup dry white wine

1 tablespoon white wine vinegar

1 tablespoon capers, minced

1 lemon slice, $^1/_2$ inch thick, seeded and minced, including peel

pinch of red pepper flakes, or to taste

$^1/_4$ teaspoon sea salt, or to taste

Rinse the chicken pieces, dry well, and trim off all excess fat. Trim any dark spots, fat, and membrane from the liver and heart and dice. Trim the tough outer layer from the gizzards and chop.

In a deep, heavy-bottomed skillet ample enough to accommodate all of the chicken pieces without crowding, warm the olive oil over medium-high heat. When it is hot enough to make the chicken sizzle, add the chicken pieces. Allow them to brown nicely and evenly on all sides, about 15 minutes. Transfer the chicken to a plate.

Drain off a tablespoon or two of the fat from the pan if the amount seems excessive. Let the skillet cool down and then place over low heat. Add the garlic, rosemary, sage, and onion all at once. Sauté until the mixture is well softened and the garlic and onion are thoroughly cooked but not browned, 5 to 7 minutes. Return the browned chicken pieces to the skillet along with the olives. Use a wooden spoon to toss all the ingredients together. Pour in the wine and add the vinegar, capers, lemon, red pepper flakes, and salt. Cover partially and continue cooking the chicken until it is tender, adding a little water if necessary to prevent it from drying out.

Transfer the chicken and its sauce to a warmed platter and serve immediately.

Ristorante Cibocchi, in a small village outside of Todi, is always filled with locals. A shopkeeper in town told me, "It's the only place where you'll find real cucina casalinga *[home cooking]." The zesty combination of chopped lemon, rosemary and sage, and local olives in this Hunter's style chicken make it delicately tart.*

Roasted Whole Suckling Pig
porchetta

The people of Lazio to the south and the Marches to the east
dispute the Umbrian claim of having invented porchetta,
but the Umbrians stand firm. Porchetta can only be made
with a suckling pig. Its beguiling flavor is the result of having
been stuffed to bursting with wild fennel, although other
herbs such as rosemary are also used. The piglet is impaled on
a sturdy skewer and affixed with prongs at each end to enable
it to turn evenly over the fire. It is then roasted slowly in a
wood-burning oven for at least four hours. Porchetta is eaten
as soon as it comes off the spit, and the eating continues
until every scrap is gone. When cool, the meat is thinly sliced,
making it suitable for a panino di porchetta, a delicious
sandwich.

*In order to prepare [Umbrian] porchetta, a young, lean pig weighing
15 to 20 pounds is procured. The pig is cleaned, opened up, and
emptied and the shoulder blades are removed. It is rinsed thoroughly
and then seasoned with a mixture of salt, ground black pepper,
garlic, wild fennel, rosemary, mint, and other herbs. The entrails
are cleaned and blanched in salt water, and then they are sliced
and dressed with the same seasonings. They are stuffed into the
pig, which is then stitched closed with sturdy kitchen string. After
the pork rind has been pricked with a knife, the pig is impaled
and spit-roasted over an aromatic wood fire.*

From Umbria Agriforeste

Sausages with Black Grapes

salsicce all'uva nera

for 4 people

8 sweet Italian pork sausages

$^1/_2$ cup water

$^3/_4$ pound seedless black or red grapes, stripped from their stems

➤ *Some place the origins of this recipe in Foligno, which lies southeast of Perugia, although it is found throughout the region. In southern Umbria, particularly in the vicinity of Orvieto and Terni, green grapes are used. In Foligno, the sausages are paired in cooking with the "black" wine grape. Locals conjecture that the dish originated during the* vendemmia, *the "grape harvest," when the fruit was plentiful and quick and hearty dishes had to be prepared to fuel those laboring in the vineyards.*

Use a sharp knife or fork to poke a few holes in the sausages before cooking them. Select a seasoned cast-iron skillet or other heavy-bottomed pan. Put the sausages and the water in the skillet and place on the stove top over medium heat. When the water has evaporated and the sausages have begun to color lightly, after about 12 minutes, add the grapes. Reduce the heat to medium-low and continue to cook the sausages, pricking them occasionally to release excess fat, until they are browned all over and cooked through, and the grapes begin to release some of their juice and soften, about 20 minutes longer. (Do not prick them too much, or they will dry out.)

Transfer the sausages and grapes to a large warmed platter, leaving behind any fat, and serve immediately.

SECOND COURSES WITH MEAT

Wood-Seared Beef Steak
bistecca alle brace

Paolo Buitoni has a cattle ranch in San Fatucchio, in the Lake Trasimeno district, where he raises Limoges cattle for meat. The animals are fed organic corn, wheat, soy, *favino* (a small black bean), and hay. While they are meant to be slaughtered between eighteen and nineteen months for maximum profit, Buitoni delays the action an additional three or four weeks to allow the meat to develop greater flavor. After slaughter, the beef is hung for three or four weeks, so that by the time it is ready for market, it is at its peak of flavor and tenderness.

An American steak can be cooked over a barbecue in the same way Buitoni cooks his unforgettable *bistecca* over a wood-fired grill: "The proper way to cook steak is to sear it first [on both sides over a wood fire] very quickly to seal in the juices; after it is cooked, season it with fine sea salt and good [extra-virgin] olive oil."

Luigi Buitoni, a nephew of Paolo, creates a more elaborate finish for his *bistecca* with this simple topping: In a skillet, warm 2 tablespoons extra-virgin olive oil over medium heat. Add 1 leek, thinly sliced, and sauté until nicely softened, 5 to 6 minutes. In a blender, combine 1 tablespoon fresh thyme leaves or 1½ teaspoons crumbled dried thyme and ½ cup extra-virgin olive oil. Thinly slice the meat and spoon some of the leek and a little thyme oil over each slice. (This amount of topping is sufficient for 2 pounds sirloin steak.)

Lamb Friccò from Gubbio

friccò di agnello

for 3 or 4 people

2 pounds boneless lamb shoulder, trimmed of excess fat and cut into cubes

$^1/_4$ cup extra-virgin olive oil

$^1/_4$ cup white wine vinegar

1 cup dry white wine

5 large cloves garlic, minced

1 tablespoon chopped fresh rosemary, or 1 teaspoon crumbled dried rosemary

1 tablespoon chopped fresh sage, or 1 teaspoon crumbled dried sage

$^1/_2$ teaspoon sea salt

freshly ground black pepper

Friccò is a typical dish of Gubbio made with lamb, veal, duck, chicken, or various types of game. The cooking method is simple, and the results succulent. The combination of wine and vinegar creates a piquant sauce, with the vinegar contributing a mild and lively sourness. How much vinegar to use depends on its strength and on the type of meat being cooked. For lamb and duck, I add between three and four tablespoons to the cooking liquid; for chicken and veal, I use a little less. Cooks will no doubt want to experiment a little, and I would recommend beginning with three tablespoons for two pounds of meat.

Rinse the lamb, then dry thoroughly to ensure that it browns properly. Select a heavy-bottomed skillet ample enough to accommodate all the meat for browning without crowding. Warm the olive oil in the pan over medium to medium-high heat. When it is hot enough to make the meat sizzle, add the lamb to the pan and brown it nicely on all sides, about 15 minutes. Stir in the vinegar, wine, garlic, rosemary, sage, and salt, mixing well. Cover tightly and reduce the heat to low. Cook until the lamb is perfectly tender, 45 to 55 minutes, removing the cover occasionally to stir well to prevent sticking. The meat is cooked when the gravy has thickened and the lamb is tender to the bite.

Season the lamb with pepper and transfer to a warmed serving dish. Serve immediately.

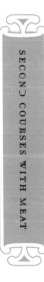

SECOND COURSES WITH MEAT

Lentils with Sausages in the Style of Cascia

lenticchie con salsicce di Cascia

SECOND COURSES WITH MEAT

for 4 to 6 people

1 pound (about 2¹/₄ cups) brown lentils, preferably Castelluccio type

5 cups meat broth

6 large cloves garlic, crushed but left whole

1 small onion, quartered

¹/₄ cup extra-virgin olive oil, or as needed

10 fresh sage leaves, or 1 tablespoon crumbled dried sage

8 sweet Italian pork sausages

3 tablespoons tomato paste

sea salt

freshly ground black pepper

⟩ *This is a typical dish of the mountain town of Cascia, to which I traveled one winter soon after earthquakes had devastated nearby towns. I arrived late at night, hungry. After tossing my luggage into an unheated room in one of the only two open hotels, I climbed up steep, worn stone steps to a little osteria where a few local people were gathered, drinking red wine. Lentils and sausages were not on the brief, handwritten menu, so I asked the waitress if she would make them for me. She was back within twenty minutes with a big plate heaped with steaming stewed lentils, which I knew from their tiny size were the cele-brated variety from nearby Castelluccio. On top rested a few plump, succulent-looking sausages.*

Pick over the lentils and rinse well. Place them in a large saucepan or soup pot and add the broth. Bring to a boil over medium heat, immediately reduce the heat to medium-low, and simmer gently, uncovered, until the lentils are half-cooked, about 15 minutes. Remove from the heat and set aside until needed.

Meanwhile, combine the garlic, onion, and ¼ cup olive oil in a wide, ample skillet. Place over medium-low heat and sauté until the garlic and onion are well softened and cooked to a deep golden color, pressing down occasionally with the wooden spoon to release some of their flavors. Do not allow them to brown. This should take 9 or 10 min-utes. Remove the garlic and onion and discard, then add the sage and stir well. Now add the sausages and brown them over medium-low heat until they are nicely colored outside and cooked through, about 20 minutes. Prick them occasionally with fork tines as they cook to release excess fat. (Do not prick them too much, or they will dry out.) Remove the sausages from the pan, cover them to keep warm, and set aside.

Use a large spoon to remove all but 2 tablespoons of the fat; if there is not enough fat, add oil as needed to equal 2 tablespoons. Stir in the tomato paste, then add the lentils and their liquid. Bring to a simmer over medium heat and cook, uncovered, until the lentils are tender and the excess liquid has evaporated, about 15 minutes. The consistency of the lentils should be somewhat fluid. Season with salt and pepper.

Transfer the lentils to a warmed platter and press the sausages into the lentils. Serve right away.

Second Courses with Fish

secondi di pesce

5

. . . Thrasymene that now
Slept in the sun, a lake of molten gold
and from the shore that once when
    armies met
rocked to and fro, so terrible
the rage, the slaughter, I had turned away
the path that led me, leading through
    a wood
a fairy wilderness of fruit and flowers
and by a brook that in the days of strife
ran blood, but now runs amber . . .

—SAMUEL ROGERS, 1763–1855

In ancient times, Lake Trasimeno was home to small lake fish, which led to the Roman expression that the Umbrians were *mangialasche*, "small fish eaters." The fish market in Umbria was naturally circumscribed, and still is, outside of the lake and the region's river areas.

Another reason for the limited consumption of fish in Umbria was that from 600 to 1861, the year of the unification of Italy, the fishermen had to pay taxes both to the Church and to the Kingdom of Italy. In 1139, the tiny Polvese Island on the lake was forced to pay the papal dominion of Perugia seven thousand tench per year, one thousand of which had to be delivered during Lent. It was customary for Trasimeno fishermen to evade the taxes by only reporting the dead fish they took from the shores. Official documents report the arrest of two Perugian women who were caught hiding fish under their skirts, the stench having given them away.

While much of the Vatican's food was produced in Umbria and transported to Rome, freshwater fish from Lake Trasimeno was a delicacy, because transporting it without spoiling required great effort and expense. Trasimeno fish were so highly prized that the papal government imposed strict regulations to assure the cleanliness of the lake and to prevent overfishing of the natural species. Nevertheless, overfishing was such a serious problem that, according to one nineteenth-century document, over sixteen thousand pounds of dace, a fish that no longer exists in Trasimeno, was fished off the shores of Passignano in a single day. Various species of fish have been introduced to the lake over the years in attempts to restock it, although not always without threatening the fragile natural balance of native species.

There are other bodies of fresh water in landlocked Umbria: Lake Piediluco; the reservoirs of Corbara and Laviano; and the Tiber River with its tributaries, the Chiasio, the Topino, the Nera, the Nestora, and the Paglia.

The fish from these freshwater sources include tench, carp, pike, eel, trout, gray mullet, and smelt, the latter two of which were introduced artificially and accidentally, respectively. Smelt has become the most sought after of the lot. *Baccalà* (salt cod) has always been popular because it could reach areas far from lake and river markets and did not have to be sold or eaten immediately. It plays an important role in many long-established festivals and religious holidays. Tagliatelle with a sauce of *baccalà* is an old tradition as well. For the dish, pieces of *baccalà* are first cooked over the embers of a wood fire before being rehydrated. They are then skinned, boned, and made into a simple sauce richly flavored with olive oil, garlic, parsley, and tomato.

The most superb large fish swimming in Lake Trasimeno is undoubtedly the carp, which in the lake district is cooked most famously *alla porchetta*, stuffed with wild fennel, pancetta, and onion and roasted over a wood fire. According to locals, the fish is only palatable when it comes from plenty of deep, clean lake water. The shallow waters, which in most areas remain at a level of six feet, don't permit the fish to swim at an energetic rate. The result of the lack of exercise causes flabby flesh and little flavor, much like what happens to chickens when they are raised in cages rather than permitted to run about the barnyard. Paolo Buitoni, whose cattle ranch is nearly in view of the lake, says that fishermen have to be very knowledgeable about the lake in order to avoid catching fish that taste like mud. The best carp fishing is during the months when there is enough rainfall to bring up the water level of the lake.

Snails
lumache

Snails are included here, although they are not fish, because neither are they meat, and they are typically purged before cooking, like mollusks. They can be eaten as an antipasto, or as a second course, cooked in a sauce.

Snails are not cultivated in Umbria, but instead are gathered in the countryside. My friend Thomas Briccetti took me to visit his horn player, Antonio Diotilevi, who lives with his mother outside the city walls of Spello. I was interested in what the *signora*, an Umbrian Jew, might cook, thinking that her cuisine was bound to include some interesting Hebrew influences. When I asked Thomas if Antonio's mother was a good cook, he dashed my notions immediately. "You're likely to find her operation more along the lines of a Roberto Benigni film," he warned me. "And don't get the idea of taking a photograph. You're bound to arrive just in time to find the *signora* giving a karate chop to the rabbit she grabbed from the backyard for the stew pot." But there were no rabbits, no *coniglio alla giudea*. Instead, Signora Diotilevi talked about snails, which were in abundance in her backyard. We ate her *bruschetta* with the oil from the first pressing of their olives, and she gave me numerous recipes for cooking land snails, a specialty of Spello. Among them was grilled snails, a dish of southern Perugia Province that fell out of favor some thirty years ago. Antonio's mother is still making it.

You can re-create the other two recipes by omitting the purging step and using high-quality canned snails in place of freshly gathered ones.

Grilled Snails
lumache sulla brace

Wash the snails and put them in a kettle with water to cover and a handful of semolina [cornmeal will do]. Let them purge for two or three days. Put them on a graticola [the square double-sided hinged hand grill] while they are still alive. Grill them on both sides until they are dead and cooked. Eat them with salt and Spello olive oil.

Snails, Hunters' Style
lumache alla cacciatora

Put the snails in a container with semolina and cover them with cold water. Purge them for two or three days. Take them out and wash them with salt and water. The snails will come out of their shells. Plunge them immediately into boiling water without salt. Drain them. Make a sughetto *with olive oil, garlic, chopped wild fennel leaves, tomatoes,* peperoncino *[hot red chile], and salt. Put the snails in the* sughetto. *Simmer it a little.*

Snails Cooked in the Manner of Suckling Pig
lumache cotte con gli aromi della porchetta

Purge the snails as for lumache alla cacciatora. *Take them out of the container and wash them with salt and cold water. The snails will come out of their shells. Wash the shells, too. Chop some wild fennel leaves or mint leaves with garlic and pancetta and mix them with some bread crumbs and olive oil (this is the* battuto). *Stuff the snails back in their shells with the* battuto. *Put them in the oven and cook them [like baked clams].*

Roasted Carp

carpa arrosto

for 1 or 2 people

1 carp, 3$^{1}/_{2}$ pounds, cleaned and well rinsed

sea salt

freshly ground black pepper

2 ounces pancetta, chopped

$^{1}/_{2}$ fennel bulb, chopped

2 large cloves garlic, chopped

3 tablespoons extra-virgin olive oil, plus oil for drizzling over the cooked fish (optional)

The colloquial Umbrian name for this famous dish is called regina in porchetta, *meaning "Queen (carp) cooked in the manner of a suckling pig." Carp is dry meat and so it needs to be prepared carefully to avoid overcooking. It also must be especially fresh for good eating. When I want to cook carp at home, I drive to Chinatown in lower Manhattan, where the fishmongers keep enormous tanks full of live carp. There, you can pick which fish looks happiest, and the seller will fish it out of the tank and kill it for you on the spot. One carp weighing approximately three pounds will satisfy one big eater, or two with moderate appetites. Although it is a big fish, its head is enormous for its size; thus to feed three or four people, look for a carp twice the size.*

Preheat an oven to 375 degrees F.

Dry the fish well with paper towels. Season the cavity with salt and pepper. Combine the pancetta, fennel, and garlic and fill the fish cavity with the mixture. Brush the outside of the fish with the olive oil.

Place the fish on a rack in a roasting pan. Measure the thickness of the fish at the thickest part, then calculate the cooking time, figuring 10 minutes per inch of thickness. Place the pan in the oven and roast the fish until it is opaque throughout when tested with a knife, about 40 minutes.

When the fish is done, remove it from the oven. Peel off the thick outer skin (it is too tough to eat), and transfer the fish to a serving platter. If you like, sprinkle some of the filling from the cavity over the fish. Check the seasoning for salt and pepper. If desired, drizzle a little extra-virgin olive oil over all. Serve immediately.

Trout with Truffles

trota al tartufo

for 4 people

$^{1}/_{2}$ cup extra-virgin olive oil

2 large cloves garlic, cut up, plus 2 large cloves, bruised

1 celery stalk with leaves, cut into several pieces

1 carrot, peeled and quartered

1 onion, quartered

1 handful fresh Italian parsley, stems, and leaves

1 teaspoon black peppercorns

1 tablespoon sea salt

4 very fresh trout, each about $^{3}/_{4}$ pound, or equivalent weight (4 pounds total) smaller trout between 8 and 12 inches in length, cleaned and well rinsed

2 black truffles, brushed clean

freshly ground black pepper

What an interesting contrast of foods in this quintessential Umbrian dish: the homely black truffle, which grows beneath the earth and explodes with aroma and flavor under the pestle, with the sweet, benign flesh of the river trout. What brings the two together is the morbidezza, *"softness," of Umbrian olive oil, which is at once gentle and full of fruit.*

Some 2 to 3 hours before you plan to cook the fish, set the olive oil to marinate with the cut-up garlic in a small ceramic or glass bowl.

When it is time to begin cooking, fill with water a fish poacher or a deep skillet large enough to accommodate the whole trout without crowding them (about 8 cups water). Add the celery, carrot, onion, the bruised garlic, parsley, and peppercorns and bring to a boil. Reduce the heat to medium and simmer for 15 minutes.

Measure the thickness of the fish at the thickest part, then calculate the cooking time, figuring 10 minutes cooking time per inch of thickness. Add the salt to the water, reduce the heat to low, and carefully lower the fish into the barely simmering water. Poach gently for the estimated cooking time minus 1 minute. The fish should be just opaque throughout when tested with a knife.

Using a large slotted metal spatula, transfer the fish to a platter. Scrape off the skin while the fish is still warm. Debone each fish carefully to remove the spine, but leave the head and tail intact.

While the fish is still quite warm, strain the olive oil to remove the garlic. In a mortar and pestle, crush and then pound the truffles directly into the infused oil and stir in the pepper to taste. Immediately spoon about half of the truffle paste onto the warm fish to keep the flesh moist and penetrate the surface with its flavor.

Serve warm or at room temperature. Spoon the remaining truffle paste over the fish to taste, or pass it at the table.

Dear Gabriella and Celina,

I drove into Todi just as all the steel blinds went down across the Italian peninsula. Boom! The signal for mass lunch throughout the country. I found a spot in the *parcheggio*, catty-corner to the Ristorante Umbria. I went in and made my way to a small table near a huge stone fireplace. There was a fire going, and just in front of it was one of those grills with four legs and a long handle that are pictured in the medieval woodcuts, set over a pile of embers. A couple ordered *trota ai ferri*. The waiter returned with raw fish, which were split open, boned, and doused with glistening green olive oil. He strewed bits of garlic and rosemary over the oil, then spread the fish, skin-side down, on the grilling rack. A few minutes later, he returned, flipped the fish onto a plate by tipping the rack, then finished cooking the trout on the other side. He did the neat trick of flipping it onto the plate again and *eccola!* That was it. I watched, mesmerized by the fire and warming my chilled toes, fingers, and face. Lots more orders for *trota ai ferri*. This is because it is the Monday after the last Sunday in February, when the fishing season for trout opens. The trout are succulent after several months of swimming in the clean, oxygenated waters of the nearby Nero River.

Now to place *my* order!

Bacioni,
Mamma

Stuffed Roasted Trout

trota farcita arrosto

for 5 people

5 very fresh trout, about ³/₄ pound each, or equivalent weight (4 pounds total) smaller trout between 8 and 12 inches in length, cleaned and well rinsed

3 tablespoons dried bread crumbs

3 tablespoons extra-virgin olive oil, plus oil for rubbing on fish

2 or 3 large cloves garlic, minced

¹/₄ cup chopped fresh Italian parsley

¹/₄ teaspoon sea salt, plus salt to taste

freshly ground white or black pepper

Despite the traditional abundance of trout in the many freshwater streams of Umbria, the fish was considered a delicacy until modern times. It was caught and sold at market, where it could fetch a good price for the fisherman. Umbrian trout are small but meaty for their size, rather than the larger variety that should be cooked more like salmon. Here is one of the many ways in which they are prepared. Be certain that the fish are thoroughly and carefully cleaned to prevent any unpleasant taste from the entrails affecting the flavor.

Preheat a broiler. Select a broiler pan that is large enough to accommodate all of the fish without crowding, to make sure each fish cooks properly. In a bowl, combine the bread crumbs, 3 tablespoons olive oil, garlic, parsley, salt, and pepper to taste. Distribute the filling evenly among the cavities of each fish. Massage the outside of each trout with enough olive oil to prevent the skin from drying out. Measure the thickness of the fish at the thickest part, then calculate the cooking time, figuring 10 minutes per inch of thickness.

Place the fish on the broiler pan and slide the pan under the broiler so that the fish is about 5 inches from the broiler element. (If using an electric oven, leave the door ajar while broiling.) Broil for half the estimated cooking time on the first side until the skin is nicely browned, then turn and baste the other side with pan juices or more olive oil and cook for about 30 seconds less on the second side. It should be opaque throughout when tested with a knife.

Remove the trout from the oven and season with salt and pepper. Serve immediately.

Viola Buitoni's Stewed Salt Cod with Tomato, Raisins, and Pine Nuts

baccalà alla Viola Buitoni

for 4 people

2 pounds salt cod fillets

$1/2$ cup extra-virgin olive oil

2 carrots, chopped

2 onions, chopped

6 celery stalks, chopped

1 bunch Swiss chard, leaves cut into julienne and stalks chopped

$1/4$ cup dry white wine

1 can (32 ounces) plum tomatoes, seeded and chopped

$1/3$ cup raisins, soaked in vinegar (any kind) for 1 hour

$1/3$ cup pine nuts

sea salt

freshly ground black pepper

about $1/2$ cup unbleached flour

corn oil or safflower oil for frying

This recipe is from Viola Buitoni, the daughter of cattleman Paolo Buitoni. It is a typical dish of the Lake Trasimeno region of her childhood. Prunes are sometimes substituted for raisins.

Until recently, salt cod, or baccalà, was difficult to find outside of ethnic markets in the United States. Now it is widely available in supermarkets, but unfortunately the refrigerated salt cod neatly resting on Styrofoam trays and covered with plastic wrap does not have the flavor or texture of salt cod preserved in the traditional manner. You may still find the more traditional product in Italian markets, and it is best to seek it out.

When buying baccalà, select meaty, white pieces rather than thin, dark ones. Stick with the skinless fillets, which cost a little more but eliminate the need for the tedious work of removing skin and small bones. The baccalà sold under refrigeration is preserved with less salt than the traditional method, and the flesh of the dehydrated fish is still somewhat soft. This reduces the soaking time substantially, usually cutting it in half. If you are using this type of salt cod, adjust the directions in the method below accordingly.

Place the salt cod in a large bowl and cover with plenty of cold water. Soak for 48 hours in the refrigerator, keeping the bowl covered. Change the water once or twice a day during the soaking, always replacing it with fresh cold water and replacing the cover. Drain the salt cod and rinse it in fresh cool water. Remove any errant skin and bones and cut the cod into 2-inch chunks, working carefully as it may crumble. Refrigerate until needed.

continued

Viola Buitoni's Stewed Salt Cod with Tomato, Raisins, and Pine Nuts
continued

In an ample, heavy-bottomed skillet, warm the oil over medium-low heat. Add the carrots, onions, celery, and chopped Swiss chard stalks and sauté until the onions are translucent and the vegetables thoroughly softened, 12 to 15 minutes. Stir in the wine, using a wooden spoon to coat the *soffritto* evenly and to deglaze the pan. Add the tomatoes, reduce the heat to low, cover partially, and simmer for a very long time until what is called *sugo finto* results, that is, a tomato sauce that is quite thick and has no water left. This should take about 1¼ hours. You will notice a layer of oxidized olive oil on top.

When the sauce is ready, drain the raisins, discarding the vinegar, and stir them into the sauce along with the pine nuts and julienned Swiss chard leaves. Mix well and simmer to heat through, about 5 minutes longer. Season to taste with salt and pepper.

Preheat an oven to 400 degrees F. Dry the salt cod well with paper towels. Place the flour in a shallow bowl or spread it out on a piece of waxed paper. Pour the corn or safflower oil to a depth of 1 inch into a deep skillet and heat over medium heat. The oil is ready when a small bit of bread dropped into the pan sizzles instantly. Have ready a platter lined with a double layer of paper towels. Just before you are ready to fry, coat the salt cod pieces in the flour, shaking off any excess.

In batches, slip the fish pieces into the oil and fry evenly on all sides until golden, about 8 minutes. Don't crowd the pan, or the fish will not fry properly and the temperature of the oil will drop. Using tongs or a slotted spatula, lift out the pieces, shaking off any excess oil back into the skillet, and transfer to paper towels to drain.

Select a baking pan and pour the sauce into it. Lay the cooked salt cod in the sauce. Slide the pan into the oven and bake until heated through, 10 to 15 minutes. Serve immediately.

Lorella Puccetti's Lentils with Seafood

zuppa di lenticchie al sapore di mare alla Lorella Puccetti

for 6 people

2 1/2 pounds mixed small mussels, and small clams

2 tablespoons, plus 1/2 teaspoon sea salt

2 pounds small squid

3/4 pound (about 1 3/4 cups) brown lentils, preferably Castelluccio type

1 celery stalk, including leaves, chopped

1 small carrot, peeled and chopped

1 onion, chopped

about 1/2 cup extra-virgin olive oil

2 cloves garlic, minced

1 cup dry white wine

1 cup peeled, seeded, and chopped canned or fresh plum tomatoes

3 tablespoons chopped fresh Italian parsley

freshly ground black pepper

Seafood is not a traditional food in the repertoire of landlocked Umbria, but nowadays it is transported from elsewhere. Lorella Puccetti, a friend from Perugia, sent this recipe on to me, which she makes for Christmas Eve. On that day, only piatti di magro, *meatless dishes, are eaten in anticipation of the abundance of food and drink on Christmas Day. The recipe is interesting because it combines mollusks and* seppie *(cuttlefish) or squid with the famous lentils of Castelluccio to create a one-pot meal. Cuttlefish are not commonly found in American markets, but squid is a fine alternative. I passed Lorella's recipe on to my friend Anna Amendolara Nurse, a well-known Italian cooking teacher, because she is famous for her own lentil and seafood dishes. She was able to buy Castelluccio lentils in her Brooklyn neighborhood (see Sources, page 157), tried the recipe out, and liked it so much that she called over a neighbor and "grabbed two people off the street" to share it with her. All reports were very pleasant.*

Rinse the mussels and clams under cold running water, scrubbing the shells with a brush. Debeard the mussels, rinse the clams and mussels again, and place them in a large receptacle. Add 1 tablespoon salt and plenty of cool water to cover. Let soak for several hours or overnight to encourage the shellfish to purge themselves of any traces of sand.

To clean the squid, separate the head and tentacles from the body by grasping the head below the eyes and pulling this top section from the body cavity. Remove and discard the ink sac from the head. Under cold running water, peel

continued

off the speckled skin. Remove the cellophanelike "spine" from the body and clean out any insides remaining in the cavity. Rinse the body thoroughly to remove all traces of ink. Cut the head from the tentacles at the "waist," above the eyes, and remove the hard "beak" from the base of the tentacles. Cut the body into rings ¼ inch wide and cut the tentacles into halves or quarters, depending upon their size. Rinse and dry the squid pieces.

Pick over the lentils and rinse well. Place them in a saucepan and add the celery, carrot, onion, and 1 tablespoon salt. Add cold water to cover by 2 inches (about 3½ cups). Bring to a boil over medium-high heat, then reduce the heat to low and simmer gently, uncovered, until the lentils are tender but still hold their shape, 30 to 40 minutes. Note that cooking the lentils gently prevents their delicate skins from slipping off. The length of cooking time will depend on the type and freshness of the lentils; if necessary, cook them further. When they are ready, drain the lentils and set them aside.

In a deep, ample skillet, warm 3 tablespoons of the olive oil over medium-low heat. Meanwhile, drain and rinse the clams and mussels thoroughly. Transfer the clams and mussels to the skillet, discarding any that do not close to the touch, and cover with a tight-fitting lid. Cook the shellfish, ensuring even cooking by tossing the pan contents occasionally while pressing on the lid to keep it in place. As soon as the shells open, after about 10 minutes, immediately remove the skillet

from the heat. Pick out and discard all the shells and transfer the mussel and clam meats to a bowl. Discard any clams and mussels that failed to open. Strain the cooking liquid through a sieve lined with cheesecloth; set aside.

Rinse and dry the skillet. Place 3 tablespoons of the oil and the garlic in a cold skillet and place over medium heat. Sauté until the oil is warmed and the garlic wilts, 3 to 4 minutes. Add the squid and ½ teaspoon salt and sauté gently until the squid is evenly opaque, about 10 minutes. Add the wine and cook for about 3 minutes to evaporate the alcohol, then add the tomatoes and parsley, cover, and simmer over medium-low heat until the squid is tender. This will take up to 10 minutes. Now stir in the drained lentils and the strained shellfish cooking liquid and simmer just to heat through and marry the flavors, about 5 minutes. Add the mussel and clam meats and toss together to heat evenly.

Remove from the heat, check for salt, and season with an additional tablespoon or so of extra-virgin olive oil and plenty of pepper. Transfer to a warmed serving dish and serve immediately.

Note: Anna has since made a successful variation of Lorella's recipe substituting cannellini beans for lentils. She soaks them overnight before cooking them and increases the cooking time to about 1 hour, or as needed.

Vegetables and Side Dishes

contorni

6

The Etruscans became rich, powerful, and independent because their
civilization was based on agriculture. Funerary urns tell the story of a
people who had a predilection for grains and vegetables, which they
liked to combine in cooking and flavor with olive oil. They were also fond
of a type of polenta, which they called *pultes*, cooked in water or milk,
flavored with garlic or onion, or combined with eggs or honey. Among
the vegetables the Etruscans ate were lettuces, wild fennel, parsley,
tarragon, garlic and onions, mushrooms, truffles, peas, and favas and
other beans that were combined with *farro* or barley in a porridge
called *farrago*. Quince compote accompanied fish, and oranges, lemons,
grapes, chestnuts, and pomegranates were eaten. But fruits from
"unhappy trees"—black figs, black raspberries, blackberries, and wild
pears—where evil spirits were believed to dwell, were taboo.

Many bean varieties were introduced by the explorers who had traveled to the New World, but there were beans in Italy during Roman
times that had been brought from Africa. A descendant of these beans,
called *fagiolo dall'occhio* (beans with eyes), still exists, and continues
to be popular in Umbria and Tuscany today. In the area of Lake Trasimeno,
where the bean is cultivated, farmers are trying to breed the original
fagiolo dall'occhio of the Romans. The beans are cooked simply by boiling
and flavored with local olive oil and salt.

There is interest among Umbrian farmers in bringing back other
ancient foods, including forgotten grains. *Farro*, emmer in English, has
returned. Lentils are an ancient, uninterrupted crop of Umbria, particularly in the mountainous areas of Castelluccio and Norcia. Colfiorito
grows lentils, too, and is also famous for its delicious, butter-fleshed,
pink-skinned potatoes.

In the spirit of things Umbrian, since the 1980s, farmers have
begun to reject modern agricultural methods for encouraging growth
and discouraging pests. Most are profoundly concerned with the whole
someness of the food they grow. Organic farming is widely practiced
throughout Umbria. The movement was initiated by the northern Italians
and the Germans, and it continues to gain followers. While Umbria
is a highly advanced region from a technological standpoint, farmers

and the general population alike are so imbued with a respect for their land and natural traditions that producing wholesome food for mass consumption meets little resistance.

Simple preparations prevail for cooking vegetables. They are often grilled or roasted, a vestige of the days when the country people virtually lived around the hearth.

Wild greens, known as *selvaggia*, are cooked in season. Traditionally, Umbria has been largely forested, unlike many other Italian regions where the land has been overcultivated for centuries. The uncultivated countryside makes it possible for many herbs and edible plants to grow wild. Rich and poor alike have always foraged for them. Wild species of celery, earth and water cresses, asparagus, arugula, *puntarelle* (chicory), hops, and myriad others flourish. Fennel, rosemary, juniper, myrtle, *cipollaccio* (wild scallions), bay, thyme, sage, and other intensely aromatic wild herbs scent and flavor the region's cooking. The many wild herbs, of which this list represents only a small fraction, also have important medicinal uses that are very much a part of mainstream pharmacology.

The deep-rooted Etruscan spiritual communion with the earth, the ancient blood that runs in Umbrian people, the region's temperate climate, and the natural resources, geological predisposition, and relative historical isolation with which Umbria has been blessed have kept it green and fertile. There is an age-old populist sentiment in Umbria that the wealth of the *proprietari* (property owners or landed classes) was based on the oppression of the *contadini* (farmers). One hears this often when talking to country people, and an Umbrian saying expresses it perfectly: *Se fai un fattore per un'anno e non ti arricchi, è meglio per te prendere una corda e t'impicchi* (If you are an overseer for a year and you don't become wealthy [by stealing from your landowner], you'd might as well take a rope and hang yourself).

Roasted Carrots and Fennel

carote e finocchi al forno

for 6 people

3 pounds carrots, peeled and ends trimmed off

3 fennel bulbs

3 tablespoons extra-virgin olive oil, plus oil for drizzling

I learned this method of roasting carrots from the chef of the sumptuous Relais Todini outside of Todi, where all kinds of vegetables are cooked on a huge open grill in the kitchen, which is visible through massive glass windows from the dining room. By spraying the carrots regularly with water as they roast, they cook to tenderness without burning, becoming a beautiful gilt orange. Prepared this way, the vegetables retain all of their sweetness and juices.

Preheat an oven to 450 degrees F. Cut the carrots in half lengthwise and then again crosswise. Trim the dark green stalks off the fennel bulbs, reserving them and the fennel fronds for another use. Now slice off the tough bottom of each bulb, and quarter the bulb lengthwise. Cut out the tough inner core from each quarter. Select 3 baking sheets and line them with aluminum foil, shiny-side up. Oil each of the foil-lined pans with 1 tablespoon of the olive oil. Place the carrots in a single layer on two of the baking sheets and the fennel quarters on the third sheet. Drizzle or brush enough additional olive oil on the carrots and fennel to ensure they are lubricated without over oiling. Using a mister, spray the carrots generously with water.

Put the pans holding the carrots into the oven and roast the vegetables for 30 minutes, spraying every 5 to 10 minutes with water. Now slide the baking sheet with the fennel into the oven to roast along with the carrots. Continue to spray the carrots but not the fennel. The carrots should be tender in about 1 hour total, while the fennel should take 20 to 30 minutes. Serve the carrots and fennel together, hot or warm.

Sautéed Mushrooms with Rosemary

funghi trifolati al rosmarino

for 4 people

 *Simple enough but typical.*

1 pound fresh wild or cultivated mushrooms

6 tablespoons extra-virgin olive oil

2 large cloves garlic, minced

2 fresh rosemary sprigs, 1 teaspoon chopped fresh rosemary, or $^1/_2$ teaspoon crumbled dried rosemary

sea salt

freshly ground black pepper

Remove any dirt from the mushrooms with a soft brush or dry cotton towel. Trim off the hard tips of the stems, but leave the stems attached unless they are very woody. Slice the mushrooms lengthwise. If they are large, cut them into quarters before slicing.

In a skillet, warm the olive oil and garlic together over medium-low heat. When the garlic has begun to soften but has not colored, after about 3 minutes, add the mushrooms and rosemary. Sauté, tossing to cook evenly, until tender but not mushy, 6 to 10 minutes, depending upon the variety (water content) of the mushrooms. Season with salt to taste and sprinkle generously with pepper. Serve immediately.

Beans with Pork Rind

fagioli con le cotiche

for 6 people

1 pound pork rind (skin)

$1/2$ cup extra virgin olive oil

2 carrots, peeled and minced

2 celery stalks, with leaves, minced

2 onions, minced

4 large cloves garlic, minced

2 cups peeled, seeded, and chopped canned or fresh plum tomatoes, or 6 tablespoons tomato paste

$1/4$ cup dry white wine

2 cups ham broth or meat broth, or as needed

6 cups drained cooked *borlotti* beans (see note below)

sea salt

> *This Umbrian version of pork and beans is from Todi, but similar dishes, called* fagiolate, *are found all over the region. Borlotti, fresh or dried, are often used, but so are fava beans, fresh or dried, and* cicèrchie (chickling peas, page 15).

In a saucepan, combine the pork rind with cold water to cover, bring to a boil, and cook for 1 hour to tenderize it and boil off some of the fat. Drain, then burn off or pull out any pig bristles that might remain in the rind. Rinse under cold running water, then cut into small dice.

In a soup pot, warm the olive oil over medium-low heat. Add the pork rind and sauté until it colors, 3 to 4 minutes. Stir in the carrots, celery, onions, and garlic and continue to sauté over medium-low to medium heat until the vegetables are softened but not browned, about 10 minutes. Stir in the tomatoes or tomato paste, mixing well, and add the wine. Cook, stirring, until the alcohol evaporates, about 1 minute. Add the broth and permit the flavors to marry for about 1 minute, then add the beans. If the mixture seems dry, add more broth. Bring the beans to a simmer and permit them to cook gently for about 10 minutes, just to bring all the flavors together. Season to taste with salt and transfer to warmed serving bowls. Serve at once.

Note: Dried beans or peas usually double in volume after rehydrating and cooking. Thus, 3 cups dried beans yield 6 cups cooked beans, although sometimes the yield is even greater. To rehydrate dried beans, place them in a bowl and cover with cold water by 3 inches. Let stand for at least 4 hours or up to overnight. Drain and rinse. (Or place in a pan with cold water to cover by 3 inches, bring to a boil, cover, and remove from the heat. Let stand for 1 hour, then drain and rinse.) Place the rehydrated beans in a pan with water to cover by 3 inches of water. Bring to a boil, reduce the heat to medium-low, and simmer, uncovered, until tender, 40 minutes to 1 hour. Season with salt only after cooking, then drain well.

Sliced Roasted Potatoes and Fennel
with Garlic and Olive Oil

patate alla porchetta

for 6 people

I adapted this recipe from a classic Umbrian one. The original calls for a bunch of wild fennel, for which I have substituted two heads of cultivated fennel, to compensate for the blander flavor.

2 fennel bulbs, with stalks and fronds intact

4 pounds boiling potatoes

$1/2$ cup extra-virgin olive oil

4 large cloves garlic, finely minced or passed through a garlic press

1 teaspoon sea salt

freshly ground medium-coarse black pepper

Preheat an oven to 375 degrees F. Select a roomy roasting pan ample enough to accommodate the potatoes and fennel without crowding.

Trim the dark green stalks off the fennel bulbs, reserving them and the fronds. Now slice off the tough bottom of each bulb and quarter the bulb lengthwise. Cut out the tough inner core from each quarter. Chop the quartered bulbs, stalks, and fronds. Peel the potatoes and cut into sticks as you would for French-fried potatoes. Pour the olive oil into the baking pan, add the garlic, and stir well together. Add the potatoes, fennel, and salt and toss together well.

Slide the pan into the oven and roast until the potatoes are tender and have a lovely deep gold cast, about 30 minutes. Remove the pan from the oven. Using a metal spatula, toss together again and place in a warmed serving bowl. Scatter with pepper to taste and serve immediately.

Viola Buitoni's Sautéed Bitter Broccoli with Potatoes

rape con le patate

for 4 people

2 Yukon Gold potatoes, unpeeled

1 bunch broccoli rabe, about 1 1/2 pounds

1 tablespoon sea salt

1/4 cup extra-virgin olive oil

4 large cloves garlic, chopped

In Italian, broccoletti di rape *and* cima di rapa *are the same vegetable, a slightly bitter relative of the turnip family. In English, the same vegetable with its florets and dark blue-green leaves is typically labeled broccoli rabe.*

In a saucepan, combine the potatoes with cold water to cover and bring to a boil. Cook over medium heat until the potatoes are tender, about 20 minutes. They should be fully tender but not falling apart when cooked. When cool enough to handle, peel the skin from the potatoes, cut them lengthwise into quarters, and then cut crosswise into medium-thin slices. Set aside.

Using a small, sharp knife, peel the skin from the tough lower stalks of the broccoli rabe (most of the bottom portion of the stalk). Cut crosswise into 3-inch lengths. Fill a large pot with plenty of water to cover the greens and bring to a rolling boil. Add the greens to the boiling water along with the salt, cover partially, and cook until the stalks are tender but not overly soft, about 5 minutes after the water returns to a boil. Drain the greens, reserving a little of the cooking liquid. Set aside separately.

In a heavy-bottomed skillet large enough to accommodate the potatoes and the greens, warm the olive oil and garlic together over low heat until the garlic is nicely softened but not colored, about 5 minutes. Raise the heat to medium and add the greens and potatoes. Stir, then raise the heat to medium-high and cook, stirring, until the vegetables are nicely coated with the olive oil and the garlic, about 5 minutes. If the vegetables appear a little dry when they are married in the pan (this will depend on the absorbency of the potatoes), add a little of the reserved cooking water as needed. Serve immediately.

Warm Chickpea Salad with Rosemary and Arugula

insalata di ceci con la rucola

for 2 to 3 people

1 cup dried chickpeas (see recipe introduction)

$^1/_8$ teaspoon baking soda

6 cups water

1 fresh rosemary sprig, about 6 inches long (optional), plus 1 teaspoon chopped fresh rosemary leaves or 1 teaspoon crumbled dried rosemary

1 teaspoon coarse sea salt

1 small clove garlic, minced

3 to 4 tablespoons extra virgin olive oil

1 bunch arugula, tough stems removed

juice of $^1/_4$ small lemon, or to taste

freshly ground black pepper

While certain canned beans can be perfectly acceptable substitutes for home cooked dried beans in some recipes, canned chickpeas acquire an unpleasant flavor from their metal container. It is advisable to rehydrate and cook a larger amount of dried chickpeas than the relatively small amount that is needed for this salad, then to refrigerate or freeze the unused portion in their cooking liquid until you need them for another purpose. This salad tastes best eaten warm, but certainly may also be served at room temperature. The arugula should be set out at the last minute, however, in order to provide a fresh and crisp bed under the chickpeas.

Pick over the chickpeas and rinse them well. Place them in a bowl with the baking soda and add water to cover by 3 inches. Cover the bowl and leave it in a cool place for 12 to 15 hours. Drain and rinse the chickpeas. Place in a pan and add the water and the rosemary sprig, if using. Bring to a boil, reduce the heat to medium, and cook until the chickpeas are tender, 1 to 1½ hours. Turn off the heat and add the salt, stirring to mix. Let stand until the salt is absorbed and the beans have cooled somewhat, about 15 minutes. Drain and set aside. You will need 2 cups cooked chickpeas.

While the beans are cooking, in a small bowl, marinate the garlic in the olive oil for about 10 minutes. For a subtle garlic flavor, strain the oil and discard the garlic. For a more assertive garlic flavor, do not strain.

Spread the arugula out on the bottom of a shallow serving bowl. In a separate bowl, toss the warm chickpeas with the garlic-flavored olive oil, the chopped fresh rosemary or dried rosemary, the lemon juice, and plenty of pepper. Arrange the chickpeas on the arugula and serve at once.

Farro and Artichokes alla Viola

farro e carciofi alla Viola Buitoni

for 4 people

1 1/2 cups *farro* (page 16)

juice of 1/2 lemon or 2 teaspoons vinegar

10 baby artichokes, about 2 ounces each

5 tablespoons extra-virgin olive oil

3 large cloves garlic, bruised

grated zest of 1/2 lemon

1/2 cup dry white wine

1 1/2 cups water or vegetable broth, or as needed

1 teaspoon sea salt, or to taste

freshly ground black pepper

Viola Buitoni gave me this recipe, which puts together two foods of which I am very fond, farro and artichokes. By birth and upbringing, Viola is firmly rooted in Umbrian soil, but her cooking is inventive. She tells me she doesn't know if farro and artichokes cooked in this manner is traditional—the method is almost like a risotto, but the result is like a thick barley soup—but this is how she makes it.

Rinse the *farro* and soak it in enough cold water to cover for about 1 hour. Rinse again and toss it well in a colander to drain and dry.

Have ready a glass or ceramic bowl filled with cold water to which you have added the lemon juice or vinegar. To prepare the artichokes, first cut off each stem flush with the base. Peel the tough skin from the stems and trim off a bit from the bottom, then slice each stem in half lengthwise. Drop the stems into the bowl of water. Using a small paring knife, tear off the tough outer leaves from each artichoke, stopping when you get to the more tender inner leaves that are yellow at the base. Using a serrated knife, cut crosswise across the top of the artichoke to remove the toughest part of the leaves. Using kitchen shears, trim away any tough parts from the top of the artichoke bottoms. Cut out the hairy choke with a paring knife. Using a large, sharp knife, cut each artichoke bottom into thin slices and add them to the bowl. Set aside until you are ready to use them.

In a large, wide skillet, warm the olive oil and garlic together over medium-low heat. Use the back of a wooden spoon to press on the garlic to force out some of its juices.

As soon as the oil is hot enough to make the artichokes sizzle, drain the artichokes and stems, pat dry, and add to the pan. Stir and toss with the garlic. When the garlic is colored but not browned, after 4 to 5 minutes, remove and discard the garlic to prevent it from imparting a bitter flavor to the oil.

Add the *farro* to the oil and "toast" it, much like you do when you add rice for risotto. Toss to coat the *farro* kernels evenly and sauté for a total of about 6 minutes or so. Then stir in the lemon zest and wine and cook to evaporate the alcohol, about 3 minutes. Add the water or broth and the salt (if you are using broth, you may not need to add more salt), and cook, uncovered, until the *farro* is tender, about 30 minutes. If necessary, add more water or broth to prevent the *farro* from drying out before it is cooked. Remember, the *farro* will be somewhat chewy, even when cooked through.

Check for salt and add pepper to taste. Spoon into a warmed serving bowl and serve hot.

Sweets

dolci

7

The Umbrians satisfy their sweet tooth by sitting in pastry shops or bars
with a *dolce* and espresso at the start of the day, and then again a few
hours after the midday meal is digested. This custom accounts for the
abundance of *pasticcerie.* Sandri, on Corso Vanucci, Perugia's main thor-
oughfare, is a particularly refined pastry shop. Its spectacular window
displays include the most famous Perugian sweets. One in particular,
torciglione, fascinates me. It is a dense, rich almond dough formed
into the shape of a serpent, or some prefer to say, the eel of the lake.
It seems to have been born around the area of Lake Chiusi, then spread
to the Lake Trasimeno district, and eventually throughout Umbria. It
is particularly pleasing to children because of its animal form, but it must
always be cut from tail end to head, a symbolic gesture of sacrifice on
the feast day.

Another famous *pasticceria* is the Muzzi bakery in Foligno, which
exports its Umbrian cakes, including *pizza dolce* and *colomba,* to the best
specialty-food shops in America. The first, which is indispensable on
Easter Sunday, has nothing in common with what Americans think of as
pizza. It is a sweet yeast bread flavored with cinnamon, candied fruit,
and *rosolio* (rose oil). *Colomba,* a sweet, buttery yeast bread formed in the
shape of a dove, is made without fruit and eaten along with *pizza dolce*
after the Easter meal. These confections are virtually never made at
home, but instead bought from the bakeries.

Umbria's two largest cities, Foligno and Perugia, both centers of
pastry and confections, have battled since ancient times about everything
from popes to sweets. The people of Foligno have always charged that
Perugians are "egocentric" and prone to abandon the interests of
the rest of the province. In terms of pastries, the feeling is that Perugians
turn their backs on local customs in an effort to appear worldly. In
any case, *pasticcerie* in towns and cities outside Perugia are more likely
to stick to the rustic desserts that are typical of the region. Bakery
sweets are made as skillfully and artistically as other crafts for which the
Umbrians are known. A walk through the back of the Muzzi shop is
like a stroll through the streets of Murano to watch the glass blowers fashion

animals and other forms. Here, bakers create swans of burnt sugar that could pass for spun glass.

Sweets are very much connected to Umbria's agricultural traditions, to its religion, and to the cycle of life. Thus, particular cakes, biscotti, and other confections are tied to holidays, to special occasions such as engagements, weddings, baptisms, and also to harvest celebrations.

Some of the more elaborate and rich confections were originally produced by *pasticcerie* for consumption by the *borghesia*, not by the common people. Today, they are bought by everyone in the finer pastry shops. Uncomplicated sweets that arose from the imaginations of the peasantry include biscotti, which made use of the almonds that grew everywhere, and sugary fritters of rice or sweetened dough. Many sweets evolved in monasteries and convents, inspired by religious themes and the contemplative life, which provided time for invention.

Both because of and despite links between particular sweets and religious holy days, there is whimsy in many of the names and their diminutives that are given to Umbrian sweets. Among them are *baci di San Francesco* (kisses of Saint Francis), *biscottini delle monache* (little nuns' cookies), *bocche di dame* (ladies' mouths), *fave dei morti* (beans of the dead), and *stinchetti dei morti* (tibias of the dead). Names like the last two may strike us as macabre, but these confections were created by sisters and brothers in the holy orders in respect for departed souls.

I have culled recipes for different categories of sweets—biscotti, fritters, cakes, candied fruits—that come from different parts of the region and which are eaten for diverse occasions throughout the year. The selection draws on different levels of skill as well. As many Umbrian sweets are purchased rather than made at home, I have followed suit here because this is a book for home cooks.

Rice and Rum Fritters of Saint Joseph

frittelle di San Giuseppe

makes about 24 fritters

2 cups milk, or as needed

1 teaspoon pure orange essence or pure vanilla extract, or 1 vanilla bean

1 tablespoon unsalted butter

$1/4$ teaspoon sea salt

$1/2$ cup short-grain white rice

2 large eggs, at room temperature, separated

$1/4$ cup unbleached flour

$1^1/_2$ tablespoons granulated sugar

$1^1/_2$ tablespoons rum

grated zest of 1 large navel orange

corn oil or safflower oil for frying

confectioners' sugar for sprinkling on fritters

The feast day of San Giuseppe (Saint Joseph) falls on March 19. This celebration of the husband of Mary is one of the most important saints' days of the Christian year. Every region celebrates the occasion with its own traditional dishes and sweets. Zeppole, Neapolitan dough fritters, are the most familiar of these celebratory foods in America, where cities with large Italian communities hold street festivals to commemorate the day. In Umbria, fritters of every kind are made at home or sold on the streets by frittellari, *"fritter vendors." The day and the fritters were always particularly meaningful when I was growing up, as the saint was the namesake of my paternal grandfather, Giuseppe della Croce.*

In a heavy-bottomed saucepan, combine the milk; orange essence, vanilla extract, or vanilla bean; butter; and salt. Bring to a simmer over medium heat. Stir in the rice, reduce the heat to low and cook, stirring constantly, until the rice is tender and has absorbed all the milk, about 20 minutes. Test the rice for doneness; if it is not tender, add a little more warm milk and continue to cook until tender but not mushy. Remove from the heat and let cool.

In a bowl, lightly beat the egg yolks until blended. In another bowl, beat the egg whites until stiff, glossy peaks form. Do not overbeat.

Stir the flour, granulated sugar, rum, orange zest, and egg yolks into the cooled rice. When the mixture is well combined, gently fold in the egg whites just until no white streaks remain.

Meanwhile, pour the oil to a depth of 2 inches into a deep, heavy-bottomed skillet and place over medium heat. The oil is ready when a bit of the fritter batter dropped

into it sizzles upon contact. Using 2 tablespoons, form
oval-shaped fritters about 1 rounded tablespoon in
size—but no bigger—and slip the fritters into the oil a few
at a time. Do not crowd the skillet. There should be
enough oil around each fritter to allow quick and even
cooking. Fry the fritters, turning them once, until cooked
through and nicely browned on both sides, about 10 minutes. Using a wire skimmer, lift out the fritters, shaking
off as much oil as possible, and transfer to a platter lined
with paper towels to drain.

Let the fritters cool somewhat, then sprinkle them with
confectioners' sugar. They can be eaten warm or at room
temperature. They also can be stored for several days,
in which case do not sprinkle them with sugar. Reheat
them in a low oven (about 300 degrees F) or bring them to
room temperature and sprinkle them with sugar before
serving.

Hot Chocolate of Norcia
cioccolata calda

for 4 people

*The hot chocolate one drinks in the town of
Norcia in winter seems thicker and hotter
than hot chocolate anywhere else. It is made
in the espresso bars and served in tiny cups
like those used for espresso, but the chocolate
is real, not like the dubious hot chocolate
one typically gets in too many establishments outside of Italy. It is important to use
the proper high-quality cocoa specified.*

3 tablespoons unsweetened cocoa
powder, preferably Perugian

3 tablespoons sugar

1 tablespoon unbleached flour

2 cups milk

In a blender, combine the cocoa powder,
sugar, flour, and milk. Process until
blended. Pour into a saucepan and warm
slowly over low heat until the chocolate
becomes dense. Serve in espresso cups
or small teacups.

Sweetheart Cake

ciaramicola

for 6 people

FOR THE CAKE:

3 whole extra-large eggs, plus 3 extra-large egg yolks, lightly beaten

1³/₈ cups granulated sugar

3 tablespoons *alchèrmes* or rum

4 drops red food coloring, if using rum in place of *alchèrmes*

1 cup fresh lard or unsalted butter, at room temperature, cut into small pieces

5 cups cake flour, sifted

1 cup potato starch

5¹/₂ teaspoons baking powder

¹/₈ teaspoon salt

grated zest of 1 lemon

FOR THE ICING:

1 egg white

1 cup confectioners' sugar, or as needed, sifted

1 tablespoon fresh lemon juice

grated zest of ¹/₂ lemon

multicolored sugar confetti or sugar sprinkles

This lovely pink cake is the most beloved of all Perugian sweets. Every family has its own favorite recipe for it. Donatella Platoni of Locanda Solomeo has four! Of course, as usual, no two recipes are the same except that all contain alchèrmes—*a compound of cochineal (a natural dye derived from desiccated beetle shells), spices, and alchohol— which imparts the rosy tint and a distinctive flavor. As this ingredient is close to impossible to find in the United States (see Sources, page 157), a mixture of rum and red food coloring can be substituted.*

Ciaramicola is associated with Easter and also with love: it is traditional for a young woman to make it for her sweetheart. The cake has become a favorite breakfast food as well, so nowadays it is available in bakeries in and around Perugia year-round. Traditionally, it is doughnut shaped, with two strips of dough laid over it in the form of a cross. Decorations vary. In some Perugian families, five little balls of dough are placed along the top bar of the cross, which then bake into the cake. These mounds correspond to the five portals of the city of Perugia: Porta Pesu, Porta Eburnea, Porta Sole, Porta Sant'Angelo, and Porta Santa Susanna. In some recipes, there are only three balls of dough, the number three being a powerful mystical symbol that represents eternal life (as does Easter). In the Buitoni family, one ball of dough is used, and it is placed at the center of the cross, to symbolize the heart of Jesus. The bakery-made cakes have no decoration at all except for the white icing and candy sprinkles.

This popular sweet is best described as a shortcake of sorts, quite dry in texture. In the past, it was always made with lard, which gave it a wonderful flavor. It is difficult to find properly rendered lard today, and most people stay away from it for health reasons. Butter is most often used in its place.

continued

Sweetheart Cake
continued

Preheat an oven to 350 degrees F. Butter an 8-inch springform cake pan and dust it with some of the cake flour, tapping out the excess.

In a large bowl, combine the whole eggs, egg yolks, granulated sugar, *alchèrmes* or rum, and the food coloring, if using. Beat with an electric mixer until a light, fluffy cream forms. Add the lard or butter and mix well. In a separate bowl, stir together the cake flour, potato starch, baking powder, salt, and lemon zest. Gradually add the dry ingredients to the bowl with the egg mixture and mix well together. You will be able to do this with the electric mixer until the mixture becomes too dry to work with the beaters. At that point, turn the mixture out onto a floured work surface and work the dough with your hands to form a uniform ball of dough, then knead until the dough is soft and silky, about 1 minute.

Divide the dough in half. Using your palms, roll one-half into a rope long enough to form a ring in the pan. It should be 1½ to 2 inches in diameter. Place it in the prepared pan, pinching the ends together. Form the remaining half into a similar rope. Cut part of this rope into 2 lengths to form a cross spanning the ring, and the remainder into 3 or 5 equal-sized portions for forming balls (see recipe introduction). Drape the rope lengths in a cross over the ring. Shape the remaining portions into balls and position them on the top bar of the cross.

Bake the cake until a skewer inserted into the center comes out clean, 35 to 40 minutes.

While the cake is baking, make the glaze: In a bowl, beat together the egg white, 1 cup confectioners' sugar, lemon juice, and lemon zest until a thick but spreadable icing forms. Add more confectioners' sugar as needed for a creamy consistency. Set aside.

Remove the cake from the oven and turn off the heat. Spread the glaze over the top of the cake while it is still in the pan and then decorate with the sugar confetti or candy sprinkles. Return the cake to the spent oven and leave it there for 5 minutes to cook the glaze without browning it.

Remove the cake from the oven, let cool completely on a rack, then remove the cake from the pan. Cut into wedges to serve.

Candied Orange Peel

candita d'arancio

makes about 3 cups diced peel

6 extra large navel oranges, well washed

water, as needed

4 cups sugar, plus sugar for sprinkling on cooked peel

2 teaspoons unflavored gelatin

If you're making these canditi, *which are so essential in Italian baking but difficult to find outside of Italy, make a good supply. Candied peel is quite simple to prepare and tastes far better than the overly sweet, nondescript "citron" that can be found occasionally, usually during holidays, in the baking section of supermarkets. Commercial citron contains food dyes, which are unnecessary. The fruits must be thick-skinned navel oranges. Grapefruit and lemons with thick skins can also be candied.*

Use a paring knife to peel the skin off the oranges, taking off all of the orange part and the underlying white pith in one or several spirals. Don't be concerned if some of the flesh comes off, too. Put the peel in a saucepan, add 6 cups cold water, and bring to a boil. Drain immediately and return the peel to the pot with 6 cups fresh cold water. Repeat boiling and draining a total of three times, which will remove the bitterness from the peel. Take care not to overboil, which will remove the pleasant citrus "bite."

In the same pan, combine the sugar and 1 cup cold water and bring to a boil over medium heat, stirring continuously and watching the pan closely to prevent burning. When the water begins to bubble and the sugar has dissolved, slip the peel into the pan and bring to a slow boil. Reduce the heat to low and cook, stirring frequently to prevent the sugar from burning. The peel is ready when the syrup becomes somewhat clear, about 15 minutes.

In a cup, mix the gelatin with 2 tablespoons cold water and let it sit for a few minutes to soften. Stir it into the pot with the peel and remove from the heat. Let cool for about 15 minutes, then use a wire skimmer to lift out the candied peel, shaking off as much excess syrup as possible back into the pan. Spread the peel out on drying racks placed over waxed paper. Sprinkle the peel on both sides with sugar until all of the visible moisture has been absorbed. Leave the peel on the racks in a cool place until the moisture has thoroughly evaporated, about 2 days.

Store the peel in a tightly closed container in a cool place. It will keep nicely for at least a couple of months. Cut the peel into small dice before using.

Almond Biscotti

tozzetti

makes about 40 cookies

1 cup sugar

3 tablespoons unsalted butter, cut into small pieces, at room temperature

1 whole large egg plus 3 large egg yolks

$^1/_3$ cup anise-flavored liqueur

grated zest of $^1/_2$ lemon

3 cups unbleached flour

$^1/_2$ teaspoon baking powder

1 cup (5 ounces) blanched almonds

These biscotti carry a subtle anise flavor from the addition of Italian anise-flavored liqueur. Hard cookies such as these are traditionally dunked into vin santo as they are eaten, but these particular biscotti are very light and good for eating alone. For dunking, good sweet Marsala can be substituted for vin santo.

Preheat an oven to 350 degrees F. Line a baking sheet with baking parchment or grease it with butter.

In a bowl, combine the sugar and butter. Using an electric mixer, beat in the whole egg until blended, followed by the egg yolks, one at a time, until creamy and lightened in color. Stir in the liqueur and lemon zest. In another bowl, stir together the flour and the baking powder. Add the flour mixture to the egg mixture and mix just until blended and a dough consistency forms. Mix in the almonds.

Shape the dough into 2 loaves, each about 3 inches wide by $^1/_2$ inch high. Transfer them to the prepared baking sheet.

Slide the baking sheet into the oven and bake until the dough is expanded and firm, about 30 minutes. Remove the baking sheet from the oven and slide the loaves onto a work surface. Let them cool for a few minutes, then, using a serrated knife, cut each loaf into slices about ¾ inch thick. Place the slices on the baking sheet, cut side down.

Reduce the oven temperature to 275 degrees F. Return the baking sheet to the oven and bake the biscotti until they are dry and lightly colored, about 30 minutes. Remove from the oven and transfer the biscotti to a rack to cool completely. The biscotti will keep up to 2 months or so in airtight tins.

A Secret Visit

A Franciscan brother in Assisi recounted
this story to me about Saint Francis:
The saint adored almond biscotti. When
he knew he was dying, he told his mes-
sengers to bring three things to him:
a cloak, candles, and almond biscotti.
A friend of Saint Francis, Lady Jacoba,
made the best almond biscotti he had
ever eaten, and it was his last wish to eat
some. Church rules forbade women to
enter a monastery, but hearing that her
beloved friend was dreaming of her
almond biscotti as he lay dying, she dis-
guised herself as a man and made her
way to his deathbed with the cookies.

La Signora
Donatella Platoni
looks out from a
window of her
country inn,
Locanda Solomeo.

Poetic Places for Sleeping and Eating

soste degne di menzione

Mark Twain, the great American writer and humorist, wrote famously about his travels in Italy. "Above all," he penned, "I don't understand why the principal architectural characteristic of Italian hotels should be that all the heat goes up the chimney and only the smoke remains in the rooms." Things have changed on the Italian hotel scene since Twain's tour of Italy—a bit too much as far as this traveler is concerned. Today, one goes to Italy and, amid the spectacle of its architecture, art, culture, and folklore, finds oneself in an American Best Western or an English Jolly hotel that serves Rice Krispies and slices of perfectly square white bread for breakfast. This happens even in Umbria. But more than many Italian regions, Umbria is also full of poetic respites for weary travelers. This book wouldn't be complete without relaying from my travels not only what I ate and where I ate it, but where I stayed in Umbria, the places that drew me in to its natural beauty, its mystical past, its splendid visions, its spirit.

This is not a directory, nor is it a sampling of accommodations. It is a personal list extrapolated from my visits to Umbria over the years.

HOTELS AND INNS

Many hotels and inns outside of major cities are closed from November to March. Reservations are advisable.

Caffèlletto, High Quality Bed and Breakfast. Via Procaccini 7, 20154, Milano. Tel: 02.3311814.820. Fax: 02.3313009. Email: info@caffelletto.it. Web site: www.caffelletto.it. An agency for exceptional accommodations throughout Italy, including Umbria. Participating homes are screened by Caffèlletto.

Hosts usually provide good breakfasts, and some offer lunch or dinner.

Hotel Miralago, Piazza Mazzini 6, Castiglione del Lago (PG). Tel: 075.951157 or 953063. Fax: 075.951924. E-mail: miralago@ftbcc.it. In the Lake Trasimeno district, a real hotel in the old style, modest but tasteful with a quiet elegance. Right on the piazza in the animated and charming town near the lake. Reasonably priced, staff very accommodating, service very good and personal.

Hotel Palazzo Bocci, Via Cavour 17, Spello (PG). Tel: 0742.301021. Fax: 0742.301464. E-mail: bocci@bcanet.it. The original building dates back to 1300, although it underwent extensive renovations during the eighteenth century, when it was converted from a palazzo to a grand residence. There are paintings by Benvenuto Crispaldi, and the wall frescoes and vaulted ceilings of the spacious sitting rooms are masterpieces. Bedrooms have anterooms with writing tables and lounges, and balconies that provide a stunning view of the valley below. Spello, whose name alone conveys its charm, is a former fortified Roman city on a steep hilltop.

La Locanda della Rocca (Country House and Restaurant), Viale Roma 4, Paciano (PG). Tel: 075.830236. Fax: 075.830155. E-mail: l.buitoni@flashnet.it. Located at the entrance of the small city of Paciano in the Lake Trasimeno district, this is more a palazzo than a country house. The current proprietor is Luigi Buitoni, and the house has been in his family for some time. Its origins, however, are medieval, although it underwent renovations

FACING PAGE:
La signora Donatella Platoni looks out from a window of her country inn, Locanda Solomeo.

during the thirteenth century. It has been modernized to provide all conveniences but retains the original elegance and grandeur of the private townhouse it once was. Outside the walls of Paciano, the countryside is immediate; from the windows of the upper floors, there are lovely vistas. Meals, prepared by Buitoni and based on local ingredients, are served in the splendid first-door dining room, or eaten alfresco in the garden in warm weather.

Le Tre Vaselle, Via Garibaldi, Torgiano (PG). Tel: 075.9880447. Owned by the Lungarotti wine family, the original palazzo was converted into an elegant hotel with a fine restaurant and an adjoining wine museum. This has been a stop for many visitors to Lungarotti's wine cellars and other travelers wanting authenticity and luxury at once.

Locanda Solomeo, Via C.A. Dalla Chiesa 1, Solomeo (PG). Tel: 075.5293119. Fax: 075.5294090. E-mail: solomeo@tin.it. The proprietors are Donatella Platoni and Pier Luigi Cavicchi, and their young son, Andrea, whose bright and engaging presence is an asset for guests with children. Their tastefully restored country house, built circa 1920, is located on the central piazza of this lazy country village that crowns a hilltop less than ten miles from the metropolis of Perugia. State-of-the art modern conveniences are found throughout the establishment, and Donatella carefully oversees the foods that are purchased for the inn, which serves breakfast, lunch, and dinner to its guests.

Relais Todini, Residenza d'Epoca, Collevalenza di Todi, Todi (PG). Tel: 075.887.521. Relais Todini is an epoch residence built on the foundations of an Etruscan-Roman structure. The splendid twelve-room villa is filled with frescoed walls, lofty beamed ceilings, and places in which to sleep, sit, eat, and

think that are a feast for the eyes and a respite for the spirit. The indoor and outdoor dining rooms have broad views of the surrounding countryside from the lofty hilltop upon which the place sprawls. Among the many luxuries are a private game park, home to everything from nearly extinct Sardinian donkeys to African zebras and Polar penguins.

Bed and Breakfast in Umbria

Bed-and-breakfast establishments have long been an alternative to high-priced hotels in Britain, Ireland, Germany, and Austria. This style of hostelry is a recent but growing development in Italy. It is a lovely way to get off the tourist route, and it can place a traveler in a town or in the countryside in private accommodations in actual homes. Bed-and-breakfast traveling can be unreliable without a guide, however, but Caffèletto (Coffee and Bed) publishes a selective detailed offering (in Italian and English) with color photographs of high-quality accommodations in every category, from farmhouses to castles, rooms to private apartments with kitchens. Booking services are provided. Caffèletto, Via Procaccini 7, 20154, Milano. Tel: 02.3311814.820. Fax: 02.3313009. Email: info@caffelletto.it. Website: www.caffelletto.it.

Agriturismo in Umbria

Farm vacations are a fast-growing cottage industry in Italy. A source for agriturismo accommodations in Umbria is *Umbria* (English Edition), a guidebook published by the Touring Club of Italy. Touring Club Italiano, Corso Italia 10, 20122 Milan. Web site: www.touringclub.it.

Eating Out in Umbria

Early travelers to Umbria found little in the way of food and wine. The era of turismo had not yet dawned. There were sparse osterie and inns that offered food when the country population was largely living from hand to mouth. Perugia, Foligno, and the valley of Spoleto were an exception. It was reported that Spoleto in particular was full of lively osterie where hard-boiled eggs, cheese, and wine were always provided. Montaigne writes of marinated fish, fava beans, peas, and artichokes in Foligno.

Today, the traveler finds beautiful food in Umbrian trattorias, osterie, inns, and restaurants. The best of these eating places are most often not in larger cities, where sheer volume and an impersonal, transitory, and often unappreciative tourist clientele discourages the purest of hearts from offering what is found in smaller, more out-of-the-way establishments. Because I have been frequently accompanied by Umbrian friends and their wide circle of acquaintances, and sometimes have been escorted by knowledgeable local officials who always know the best spots, I have been fortunate to find myself in many places where authentic local dishes are served.

Aladino, Via delle Prome 11, Perugia (PG). Tel: 075.5720938. A pleasant and relaxed restaurant that focuses on seasonal ingredients and regional foods. The cooking doesn't stray from authentic local dishes, which are executed with a delicate hand.

Cesarino, Via della Gabbia 13, Perugia (PG). Tel: 075.5736277. Located on a little side street off Perugia's central piazza, this is a perfect spot for no-frills Umbrian cooking. The place is always packed with locals, the waiters have been there since the beginning of time, and the food is as close to home cooking as one can find in a restaurant.

Da Faliero, Località Montebuono, Magione (PG). Tel: 0758.476341. My friend Viola Buitoni brought me to this lively, informal trattoria near Lake Trasimeno.

The place is always full of locals and there are tables for eating outdoors and space for dancing. This is where travelers should go for authentic torta al testo (griddle bread), because here it is made in the traditional way, baked in a huge, open wood-fired oven in the center of the restaurant. Even the local phone book recognizes the superiority of the torta, as evidenced by the statement that follows the number: *"la torta de la Maria è la più bona che ce sia"*—"Maria's torta is the best there is." Typical local first courses, fish from Lake Trasimeno, and beans with ham are among the long list of good, homespun dishes.

Gio' Arte e Vini, Via Ruggero d'Andreotto 19, Perugia (PG). Tel: 075.5731100. An important aspect of the restaurant is the *enoteca*, which has an extensive and extraordinary wine cellar. The restaurant is equally extraordinary. On the first level are *servizi informativi,* that is, informative services to the clientele about wines, spirits, olive oils, and vinegars. The reasonably priced menu is thoroughly Umbrian, drawing on the specialties of the region.

Il Bacco Felice di Salvatore Denaro, Via Garibaldi 73, Foligno (PG). Tel: 0742.341019. Salvatore Denaro is an expansive Sicilian with a passion for wine and food. His place is both an enoteca, because it specializes in wines and houses an enormous choice of superb vintages, and a trattoria. The earthy but skillfully prepared food, with its focus on quality local products, meets the high level of wines.

Il Convento, Corciano (PG). Tel: 075.6978946. As the name implies, Il Convento was once a convent, and like most convents and monasteries, it is situated in a lovely spot. At the foot of the medieval hill town of Corciano, with a pretty view of the valleys below, it provides for contemplation of the spirit and the flesh.

The restaurant's menu carries all local specialties, including typical Umbrian spit-roasted meats and game.

La Fontanella, Via Bernardo da Quintavalle 7/b, Assisi (PG). Tel: 075.813048. The proprietors, Francesca and Marco Francalancia, run this small and informal secluded garden cafe behind the stone walls of one of Assisi's highest high-altitude streets. It is hidden on one side by stone walls, while the other side faces the spectacular panorama of the valleys far below this summit of the Assisi hills. They serve lovely drinks and cocktails; *gelati, antipasti,* panini, and *stuzzichini* (nibbles) from March to September. The building dates back to at least medieval times, and the original kitchen is virtually intact.

La Locanda della Rocca. See location and description, page 147.

Le Tre Vaselle. See page 148. Tel: 075.9889129. The celebrated restaurant features special meals and foods on saints' days and other significant Umbrian feast days. There are dinners around a grand fireplace in winter, and the Christmas season festivities are especially lovely. These include a *cena della vigilia,* the traditional Christmas Eve fish dinner; an elegant Christmas Day breakfast and dinner; and a gala New Year's Eve dinner. Lungarotti wines are served with every course.

Locanda dell'Angelo, Viale XXV Aprile, Ameglia (PG). Tel: 0187.64391. Angelo Paracucchi, the Umbrian-born chef who has become a legend in his own time, operates a restaurant and offers accommodations in this country inn near Spoleto. He and his wife, Francesca, do the cooking themselves. The food is Umbrian at heart, although some dishes are clearly influenced by Paracucchi's experi-

ence abroad and are carried out with a creative hand. The cooking reflects an impassioned attention to detail and a reverence for the region's superb olive oil and other fine products.

Osteria dell'Olmo, Strada Olmo, Stazione di Ellera 8, Perugia (PG). Tel: 075.5179140. Just outside of the city walls in an elegant villa built in the 1600s. Wonderful antipasti are served here, and the other courses, all featuring regional fare, are also superb. The restaurant is patronized by businessmen and local society year-round and in the summer by tourists.

Osteria del Bartolo, Via del Bartolo 30, Perugia (PG). Tel: 075.8010281. This restaurant is highly touted for its impeccable and beautiful Umbrian food, although the kitchen departs from tradition with many dishes. Bread is baked fresh every day.

Ottavius, Via del Gonfalone 4. Tel: 0742.360555. At the entrance of the enchanting town of Bevagna. Bevagna was a strategically located Roman town once, and the influence of Rome is still felt here, both culturally and gastronomically. Signora Edelweiss Biagetti, the proprietor of this pleasant restaurant, is most accommodating and welcoming to whomever dines in her place, and there is a warm, cozy feeling here. The food is terrific, very clearly with a taste of Rome: some of the dishes are fiery, as Lazio would have it, touched as they are with hot red pepper. Dishes like *paiata di vitellina* (a tasty fry-up of the intestine of milk-fed veal) and *trippa di vitella alla romana* (Roman-style tripe) are unabashedly Roman dishes, but they are as much Bevagna dishes. For those who are not inclined toward the "variety meats" the Roman kitchen loves so much, there are plenty of offerings on the menu to appeal to every taste.

Relais Todini. See page 148. The food here is organic and, in keeping with the elegance of the residence, refined in its delivery. The beef comes from cattle raised on Todini's ranches in Argentina, and many of the other foodstuffs are produced on the estate.

Ristorante La Piazzetta, Via Deliziosa 3, Perugia (PG). Tel: 075.66012. A large, beautiful restaurant tucked into a residential back street on a descent from the Corso Vanucci in Perugia. Run by Lea Baldoni, a descendant of one of Perugia's old families, the restaurant offers a mixture of creative cooking and typical Umbrian dishes. *Strangozzi* and certain other local specialties are always on the menu, but the chef likes to be inventive, too.

Ristorante Umbria, Via S. Bonaventura 13, Todi (PG). Tel: 075.8942390. Whoever comes here will be sure to find good, authentic local cooking and fresh, seasonal ingredients, such as fresh porcini in September, wild greens, and freshwater fish. Fausto Todini, the owner and chef, cooks *cicèrchie* (chickling peas), fava beans, local lentils, and other foods that are typical, local, and genuine. A long terrace, open in warm weather, faces a beautiful vista of surrounding hills and valleys. In cold weather, sit by the huge fireplace where the waiters cook fish and meats as they are ordered.

Settimio, Frazione San Feliciano, Via Lungolago 1, Magione (PG). Tel. 075.8476000 or 075.849104. This is where local inhabitants send you for *tegamaccio* (fish stew), eel, poached perch fillets, lake shrimp fry, risotto with perch, and other fish dishes of the Trasimeno district. There are also regional desserts and some good local wines. The trattoria is at the lake's edge and always full.

Taverna, Via delle Streghe 8, Perugia (PG). Tel: 075.5724128. Housed in several beautifully restored rooms in an ancient palazzo in the city center, the restaurant serves the provincial cooking of Perugia and modern renditions of ancient dishes.

Trattoria Camesana, Castello di Pissignano, Campello sul Clitunno, Lizori (PG). Tel: 074.3520340. The local press calls the owner "the muse of song and the nymph of Clitunno," and her cooking "so *gustosa*, so appetizing, so bright and pleasant, so seductive." Daniela Bottoni is a young, creative chef-owner devoted to "living cuisine," in which only fresh, wholesome, local ingredients are used.

Trattoria Lea, Via S. Florido 38, Città di Castello (PG). Tel: 075.8521678. E-mail: lea@omniait.com. Without a doubt, this is one of my favorite restaurants in all of Umbria for its impeccably fresh and lovely homemade food. The warm, lively dining room is full of noisy local families. Eating here nearly duplicates the feeling of eating in an Umbrian home where the *signora* of the house is a superb cook. The cook-owner is Lea Gianbanelli. Her husband and her daughter, Michela, help out in the kitchen and dining room.

Villa Roncali, Via Roma 25, Foligno (PG). Tel: 0742.391091. A restored Renaissance villa transformed into an upscale establishment, this restaurant offers elegant food based on local high-quality meats, cheeses, and produce. I was once invited to Villa Roncali for a sumptuous multicourse dinner attended by at least one hundred people, but the food showed none of the signs of cooking for mass feeding.

Festivals

sagre

Festivals are epidemic throughout Italy, and Umbria, steeped in mystical, agricultural, and artistic traditions, has more than its share of them.

JANUARY

Montefalco: January 6, Awaiting Befana (the Italian Saint Nicholas) event and a children's carnival.

Trevi: January 27, Procession for Saint Emiliano (patron saint). The townspeople carry the emblems of the Arts and Crafts Guilds through the streets.

FEBRUARY

Norcia. Nursino carnival, held since the seventeenth century and celebrated in masks, with music, dancing, and a fox hunt; last weekend in February, Black Truffle Festival and exhibitions of local *salumi,* cheeses, and other typical products.

MARCH

Umbertide: March through May, Jazz Festival.

APRIL

Bettona: Good Friday, torchlight procession.

Bevagna: Easter Sunday, Race of the Risen Christ.

Cascia: Good Friday, Procession of the Crucified Christ (dates back to the twelfth century).

Castelluccio di Norcia: Last Sunday in April, Feast of Flowering, a celebration connected to the return of the sheep to the mountains, with roots in Etruscan times.

Castiglione del Lago: First Sunday of April, Tulip Festival; April through September, on the third Saturday of each month, the Summer Collectible and Antique Market.

Città della Pieve: Easter Monday, wine-spouting fountains and the Festival of the Easter Cheese Bread and Chestnuts.

Gualdo Tadino: Last Sunday in April, Feast of May, reenactment of the feast of 1100.

Montefalco: Oenological Week coincides with Easter week, with demonstrations by wine makers and a wine market; Holy Saturday, reenactment of the Resurrection of Christ.

Montone: Feast of Easter Monday.

Narni: Historical Opening of the Taverns.

Orvieto: Sunday after Easter, Festival of Wood Pigeon (celebration of wild game).

Terni. Singing procession with a night procession of allegorical floats.

Todi: Antique Show of Italy, coincides with Easter.

MAY

Alviano: First Sunday in May, Feast of Farmer Saint Isidoro.

Cascia: Third Sunday in May, Feast of Saint Rita (patron saint); May 22, historical parade in medieval costumes and the Blessing of the Roses.

Castiglione del Lago: May 1, Let's Paint the Sky (Kite) Festival.

Gualdo Tadino: First Sunday of May, Palio of the Crossbow; last week in May, Mountain Flowers Festival.

Passaggio: Second Saturday in May, Fair of the Saint (Crispolto), revolves around the sale of horses, goods, and wares to commemorate the town's origins as a marketplace.

Gubbio: Race in honor of Saint Ubaldo; crossbow competition.

Orvieto: Feast of the Dove on the day of Pentecost.

San Gemini: Porchetta (Roasted Pig) Festival.

JUNE

Assisi: Second Saturday in June, Feast of Corpus Christi, with an *infiorata*.

Bettona: Second Saturday in June, traditional *infiorata* and Corpus Domini procession.

Bevagna: June 6, Feast of Saint Joseph and Blessed Giacomo Bianconi; June 20 to 30, festival during which the city is ruled by citizens in costume, old trades (paper making, rope making, basket making) are practiced along the streets, and contests between various town factions are held. The taverns serve food prepared from old, unusual recipes.

Castiglione del Lago: Last week in June, Trasimeno Quality Market, at which traditional local handicrafts and agricultural products are demonstrated, exhibited, and sold.

Città della Pieve: June 19 to 21, Feast of Saint Louis, celebrated with an *infiorata*; Snail Festival at the Tavern of Torre del Vescovo.

Gualdo Tadino: Third Friday in June, Night of Fire and the Guazza of Saint JoAnne is reenacted in thirteenth-century costume.

Sigillo: Strawberry Festival.

Spello: June 10, Feast of the Corpus Christi, with an elaborate *infiorata*.

Spoleto: June through October, Festival of the Two Worlds (music and theater).

Torgiano: June 10, *infiorata*.

JULY

Aquasparta: July through August, Festival of Water.

Castiglione del Lago: International Choir Music Review; International Folklore Review, and the Amatory Theater.

Passignano: Last Sunday in July, Palio of the Boats and Race of the Jugs. The race, run by women in nineteenth-century costume with jugs of water balanced on their heads, commemorates local women who bravely transported water from outside the fortified city to safety within the city walls during wartime.

Trevi: Throughout the summer until September, various food festivals.

AUGUST

Assisi: Festival of Forgiveness, Festival of Saint Ruffino (patron saint) and of Saint Chiara.

Bettona: First week, Festival of the Roasted Goose and local gastronomy in the central piazza; Festival of Hospitality, various gastronomic festivals throughout the area to celebrate local specialties.

Corciano: Dedicated to the work of artists, theater, and music; August 15, reenactment in fourteenth-century costume of everyday aspects of medieval life.

Città della Pieve: Palio of the Terzieri (horse race in the historic center) begins after the opening competition on August 15.

Gualdo Tadino: August through September, International Competition of Ceramic Arts.

Gubbio: Palio delle Contrade.

Montefalco: August 12 to 14, Run of the Oxen, a reenactment of the ancient tournament between the four factions of the town.

Montone: Second week of August, tournaments, bow competitions, and other games and public serenades.

Nocera Umbra: August 10 to 20, Water Festival, with musical events in the historic center.

Passignano: Mid-August, Joust of Arrigo, the city's namesake, in gothic costume.

Solomeo: Festival of Strozzacaponi (Crostone).

Spoleto: August 5, Annual Village Feast in Assunta.

Todi: August through September, Festival of Todi.

Torgiano: Local food festivals with music and art are held throughout the month of August; August is "wine color" month, during which local artists dip their watercolor brushes in Torgiano wine instead of water.

Trevi: First three weeks of August, Trevi in the

Piazza/Dinner in the Piazza, when the town offers local specialties for outdoor dining.

September

Cannara: Onion Festival.

Deruta: Festival of Summer's End, with art exhibitions, theater, concerts, and gastronomical events.

Foligno: September through October, festivals of the red potato of Colfiorito.

Gualdo Tadino: Last week in September, Games and Gates Show, with a parade in Renaissance costumes and various Renaissance games and sports.

Montefalco: Grape Festival; Honey Show and Market.

Nocera Umbra: Convention of Hot Springs, celebrates the therapeutic properties of the local water and white clay, used since ancient times. First Sunday, Cavalcade of Satriano reenacts the last trip of the dying Saint Francis, made from his hovel in Nocera to Assisi. Second Sunday, a festival of the products of the Apennines region.

Panicale: First Sunday, Feast of Saint Pellegrino (patron saint); grape festival.

Passaggio: Second Friday in September, Fair and Festival of Our Lady of the Bridge.

Passignano: The city uses its two-hundred-kilogram skillet, the largest in the world, for its annual Fish Festival of local catch.

Umbertide: Ecological Agricultural Fair.

October

Assisi: National celebration in honor of Saint Francis.

Cannara: Wine Festival in Collemancio.

Massa Martana: October 30, Feast of San Felice; Black Truffle Festival.

Montone: End of month, Feast of the Woods for celebrating local products, including mushrooms and truffles.

Perugia: Chocolate Festival.

Trevi: First Saturday, historical parade of the Palio of the Tertiary, with a procession in historical costumes; second Sunday, Gastronomic Market and Show; third Sunday, Celery and Sausage Festival; fourth Saturday, Scenes of Medieval Life, with dramatizations. Throughout the month, shows with gastronomical and folkloric themes are held in the historic center.

November

Città di Castello: Truffle exhibitions.

Deruta: Last Saturday in November, Potters' Feast on the feast day of Saint Catherine of Alexandria (patron saint), and afterward, feasting in the piazza on chestnuts, *torcolo* (fruit yeast bread), and high-quality local wine.

Panicale: Festivals throughout November for local products from the woods, and also local chestnut desserts during the *castagnata* (chestnut harvest).

Perugia: Feast of the Dead.

Torgiano: Throughout the month, Banquet of Italian Wine Tasting.

December

Basqui-Terni: December 6, Feast of Saint Nicolas (patron saint).

Bevagna: December 6, children of Bevagna receive gifts and traditional confections.

Cannara: December 25, The Bonfire.

Castiglione del Lago: Throughout the month, streets and piazzas are decorated for Christmas.

Gualdo Tadino: Show of herbs and medicinal plants from local woods.

Magione: Second Saturday in December, Fishermen's Festival.

Classes in Umbrian Cooking

In the United States

La Vera Cucina: Julia della Croce's Italian Cooking School, Rockland County, NY. Toll-free: 877.443.8580, pin 2330, or 845.634.3172. Web site: www.juliadellacroce.com.
E-mail: julia@juliadellacroce.com. Specializing in Italian regional cooking. Instruction by award-winning cooking teacher Julia della Croce, and celebrated guest teachers of Italian and Umbrian cooking. Classes in wine appreciation. Referral service for professional Italian chefs, Italian food consultants, Italian food and travel photographers, and Italian food, wine, and olive oil experts.

The Magazine of La Cucina Italiana Cooking School, 230 Fifth Avenue, New York, NY 10001.
Tel: 212.725.8764, toll-free: 888.742.2373. E-mail: piacere@earthlink.net. Demonstration classes with well-known Italian chefs and cookbook authors. Classes in wine and olive oil appreciation.

In Italy

To Italy with Julia: Toll-free: 877.443.8580, pin 2330, or 845.634.3172. Web site: www.juliadellacroce.com. E-mail: julia@juliadellacroce.com. Unique culinary and cultural tours with Julia della Croce, award-winning author-teacher. Regularly scheduled tours and custom tours to Umbria and Italy.

Cucina Viva, Campello sul Clitunno (Spoleto). E-mail: cultura.viva@libero.it or jlibri@aol.com. U.S.A. contact: Forktales, Inc. Tel: toll-free 877.443.8580, pin 2330. Fax: 845.634.0244. Cooking classes in Umbria; accommodations in restored country villas. Courses include trips to local markets; cheese, olive oil and wine producers; norcini (makers of sausages, prosciutti, *salumi* and other meat specialties); authentic regional restaurants serving typical specialties from locally grown foods; Deruta and Gubbio pottery artisans; local markets for needlecraft, embroidery, lace, linen, and tapestry handicrafts; copper and wrought-iron artisans.

Locanda dell'Angelo di Paracucchi. See page 150. Famed chef Angelo Paracucchi operates a cooking school in Trevi. Contact him at his inn.

La Locanda della Rocca. See page 147. Luigi Buitoni gives cooking classes in the kitchen of his splendid inn.

Coluccio & Sons
1220 60th Street
Brooklyn, NY 11219
Tel: 718.436.6700
Italian and Umbrian food specialties. Product list available. Orders shipped.

Dairy Fresh Candies
57 Salem Street
Boston, MA 02113
Tel: 1.800.336.5536
Fax: 1.617.742.9828
E-mail: j.j.reilly@verizon.net
Web site: www.dairyfreshcandies.com
Source for *alchèrmes* and baking supplies.

Dean & DeLuca
Mail-Order Department
560 Broadway
New York, NY 10012
Tel: 212.431.1691, 800.221.7714
Kitchen equipment; Italian specialty foods.
Catalogue available.

Di Palo Italian Fine Foods
206 Grand Street
New York, NY 10013
Tel: 212.226.1033
This "Old World" grocery in New York City's Little Italy (according to Louie DiPaolo, "the twenty-first region of Italy") since 1925, carries every Italian food specialty exported. Will ship any product ordered by phone.

Gallo Brokerage
93 Willow Street
Wilkes-Barre, PA 18702
Tel: 570.882.9743
Fax: 570.822.6622
Broker for Italian specialty foods, supplying distributors and importers.

Buon Italia
79 9th Avenue
New York, New York 10011
Tel: 212.633.9090
Fax: 212.633.9717
E-mail: info@buonitalia.com
Web site: www.buonitalia.com
Italian and Umbrian food specialties. Discriminating product list. Wholesale and retail. Same-day delivery in New York City; overnight shipping nationwide.

That Fine Italian Hand
166 Ridge Road
New City, NY 10956
Tel: 845.634.3172, toll-free 877.443.8580/pin 2330
Fax: 845.634.0244
Mail order for original signed works of art including photographs by Umbrian and Italian artists; Umbrian and Italian handicrafts by mail order.

Acknowledgments

Above all, to Lorella Puccetti for her intelligence and generosity and the many days she devoted to my research in Umbria. To Gabriella and Celina for the gleeful and love-filled welcomes whenever I return. To Donatella Platoni of Locanda Solomeo for beautiful food and gracious hospitality. To Pier Luigi Cavicchi and Umbria Export for guidance and assistance, and to young Andrea Cavicchi for particularly charming company. To my editor, Bill LeBlond, for the opportunity to write this book. To my agent, Judith Weber, for smoothing out the wrinkles. To Sharon Silva, my hands-on copy editor for particularly hard, patient work. To Francesco Sacchini, for his generosity with the Italian copyediting and for the speed with which it was delivered. To my mother, Giustina Ghisu, and to my sister, Justine Kadoche, for help with recipe testing. To Emily Shachter, my *angelo custode*—"guardian angel." To Flavia Destefanis for many kindnesses and contributions. To Paolo Destefanis, *bacioni* for the leads in Umbria. To my elegant aunt, Rita Ghisu, for her prayers, great stories, and laughter along the way. To John and Catherine Walber for their extraordinary support and friendship. To award-winning journalist Bill Marsano for his friendship, remarkable generosity, and the default trip to Trevi *(grazie mille)*. To Viola Buitoni for starting me off on the right foot, and for many kindnesses. To Clarisse Schiller for producing marvelous photo opportunities; *ti abbraccio*; here's to a lifetime of friendship under the Umbrian sky. To Paolo Buitoni and Silvia Buitoni for their hospitality. To Sonia Marini of Umbria Export for much research on my behalf. To Oswaldo Herrara for help with recipe testing, especially *torta al testo*. To Rita Boini, Umbrian journalist and author, for sharing so much of her professional knowledge and for notes about Umbrian wines. To Guglielma Corsi for teaching me so much through her books and for putting up with a photo session. To Ernie Symanski for the many hours testing the most esoteric recipes, for the reruns of *ciarami-cola*, and for the *alchèrmes* in the lab that was above and beyond the call of duty. To Mary Ann Castronovo Fusco for tenacity in trying out *ossa dei morti*. To Nick Malgieri, friend and pastry wizard, for enlightenment about meringue pastry. To Olga Urbani and Carlo Urbani for the warm welcome to chilly Norcia in February and for an education on truffles; also to Luigi Ciciriello for the truffle wisdom. To Jack Ubaldi, and to Philip Martino, master butchers from the old school, for their expert advice on all meat matters. To La Molisana pasta for the stock of *bucatini* for recipe testing. To Bertolli USA for the gallons of *olio*. To Luigi Buitoni, the late Professore Pizzardi, Antonio Diotilevi and Signora Diotilevi, Elsa Jean Davidson, Anna Amendolara Nurse, Lea Baldoni of La Piazzetta in Perugia, and Lea Gianbaldini of Trattoria Lea in Città di Castello, each for his or her contribution to this book. To Dr. Rudolfo Cortellini and Natale La Cammara of Istituto Nazionale per il Commercio Estero (ICE–Rome), deep thanks for the education in olive oil and the grand tour of Umbria. Thanks as well to Angelo Infusino (ICE–Perugia); Paul Caccia (ICE–Québec); Prof. Gian Franceso Montedoro; Prof. Agostino Tombesi; Prof. Maurizio Servili; Dr. Paolo and Signora Rapanelli; Carlo Antonini, mayor of Trevi; Bruno Bini, mayor of Bevagna; Domizio Natali, mayor of Campello sul Clitunno; Guido and Ernesto Guidobaldi of the Guido Baldi Olive Oil Company; Prof. Silvano Piatti of Bevagna; Relais Todini; and Antico Frantoio Carlo Carletti in Campello sul Clitunno. To Mary Ann Esposito for finding an American source for *alchèrmes*. Also thanks to Judy Ridgway (London) for her engaging company on the olive oil trail in Tuscany and Umbria and for sharing her vast knowledge about olive oil with me.

Index

Table of Equivalents

The exact equivalents in the following tables have been rounded for convenience.

Liquid/Dry Measures

U.S.	METRIC
¼ teaspoon	1.25 milliliters
½ teaspoon	2.5 milliliters
1 teaspoon	5 milliliters
1 tablespoon (3 teaspoons)	15 milliliters
1 fluid ounce (2 tablespoons)	30 milliliters
¼ cup	60 milliliters
⅓ cup	80 milliliters
½ cup	120 milliliters
1 cup	240 milliliters
1 pint (2 cups)	480 milliliters
1 quart (4 cups, 32 ounces)	960 milliliters
1 gallon (4 quarts)	3.84 liters
1 ounce (by weight)	28 grams
1 pound	454 grams
2.2 pounds	1 kilogram

Length

U.S.	METRIC
⅛ inch	3 millimeters
¼ inch	6 millimeters
½ inch	12 millimeters
1 inch	2.5 centimeters

Oven Temperature

FAHRENHEIT	CELSIUS	GAS
250	120	½
275	140	1
300	150	2
325	160	3
350	180	4
375	190	5
400	200	6
425	220	7
450	230	8
475	240	9
500	260	10